A PRACTICAL

SYSTEM OF BOOK-KEEPING

BY

SINGLE AND DOUBLE ENTRY:

CONTAINING

FORMS OF BOOKS AND PRACTICAL EXERCISES,

ADAPTED TO THE USE OF

THE FARMER, MECHANIC, MERCHANT, AND PROFESSIONAL MAN.

TO WHICH IS ADDED

A VARIETY OF USEFUL FORMS FOR PRACTICAL USE, VIZ.: NOTES, BILLS, DRAFTS, RECEIPTS, ETC., ETC.: ALSO, A COMPENDIUM OF RULES OF EVIDENCE APPLICABLE TO BOOKS OF ACCOUNT, AND OF LAW IN REFERENCE TO THE COLLECTION OF PROMISSORY NOTES, ETC.

BY

LEVI S. FULTON AND GEO. W. EASTMAN
AUTHORS OF A COMPLETE SYSTEM OF PENMANSHIP.

REVISED EDITION.

TROY, N. Y.:
PUBLISHED BY H. B. NIMS & CO.,
NEW YORK: A. S. BARNES & CO.,
AND SOLD BY THE PRINCIPAL BOOKSELLERS THROUGHOUT THE UNITED STATES.

BOOK-KEEPING BLANKS,

NEATLY RULED ON FINE PAPER, AND PUT UP IN THE MOST CONVENIENT FORM FOR USE: ADAPTED TO FULTON AND EASTMAN'S BOOK-KEEPING.

I. ACCOUNT-BOOK FOR THE FARMER. One book.
II. DAY-BOOK AND LEDGER FOR THE MECHANIC. Two books.
III. DAY-BOOK, JOURNAL, AND LEDGER FOR THE MERCHANT. Three books.

The use of the above Blank Books will bè found very important, in familiarizing the Scholar with the Forms relating to the Keeping of Accounts, according to FULTON and EASTMAN'S System of Book-keeping.

Persons sending for these Blanks will please specify in their orders the number they want of each kind.

CONTENTS.

BOOK-KEEPING.

PREFACE.

Book-keeping is a mercantile term, used to denote the method of keeping accounts of all kinds, in such a manner that a person may at any time know the true state of his affairs.

Every person, engaged in business for himself, should keep a book of some kind in which to record all his business transactions. The day-laborer, the farmer, and the mechanic, should keep an account with every person with whom they deal. No one should trust transactions of a pecuniary nature to his memory alone.

The merchant who is incompetent to keep a full and accurate record of his business transactions, or neglects to do it, must abandon all claims to the confidence which he might desire others to repose in him; all hope of success in the accumulation of property; and forego all peace of mind, which he might otherwise enjoy, in the prosecution of his business.

* * * * * * * * * *

Book-keeping should be more extensively taught in our schools. Among the many books already published on this subject, none are well adapted to, and very few, if any, are intended for, the use of common schools. Hence, this important study is almost entirely neglected by those who attend such schools only, and pursued by but few who attend those of a higher grade.

Many, indeed, think that the study of Book-keeping is useless, unless pursued in the counting-room, or in connection with the actual business of buying and selling. This is a great mistake. Book-keeping is one of the most important branches of study that can be pursued by those of suitable age and attainments in our schools of every grade. It is a highly important branch of female education, and should be ranked next in the course of study, and next in importance, to reading, writing, and arithmetic. As well might a person postpone the study of arithmetic until he has occasion to cast the interest on a note, or to use a knowledge of figures for any other purpose, as to defer the study of Book-keeping till he has the cares of actual business on his mind. In fact, while the pupil is pursuing this study, he is applying the principles of arithmetic in a most practical manner. He is gaining discipline of mind—as much, at least, as by any other study. He is learning to spell the names of a great many articles in commerce, which would not otherwise come under his notice. He is, or may be, improving his style of penmanship, especially when, as in this work, all the items, which he is required to copy, are printed in a beautiful script type. By taking such a view of the subject, we are led unhesitatingly to assert, that the school-room is the place to study Book-keeping; and, with a suitable teacher and text-book, a thorough knowledge of it can be obtained there.

Such a text-book the Authors confidently believe they now submit to the public.

The work is divided into three parts. Part First embraces three forms, or methods of keeping accounts, adapted to the use of particular classes of individuals, and suited to the different capacities of students.

After each form is a practical exercise, designed to test the learner's knowledge of the form he has just passed through, and which cannot fail to give as thorough and practical a knowledge of Book-keeping as could possibly be obtained in a counting-room.

The following are some of the advantages of the "Merchants' Form" over that generally used by them, where the Journal is a mere copy of the Day-Book or Blotter, and where each entry, or all those on the same page of the Journal, are separately posted:

It saves more than one-third of the writing in journalizing. It saves at least three-fourths the labor in posting. It requires but twelve lines in the Ledger to post a year's business, while in the ordinary way as many pages may be necessary. In settling with a person at the end of a year, you have only to refer back to twelve places in the Journal to show him all the items of his account, whereas in the ordinary manner of keeping books you might have to refer to five hundred.

Other advantages might be named, but these are deemed sufficient to mention here.

Part Second contains a clear and comprehensive exposition of the principles of Double Entry exemplified in two sets of books, the second of which is peculiarly adapted to a retail business; and as double entry is the only method that can be relied on for accuracy, it is confidently believed that this form of books, when known, will be generally adopted by that class of merchants for whom it is designed.

The Third Part was prepared by a member of the bar, and the authorities consulted, and from which the rules here laid down were collected (in addition to the reports of our Supreme Courts), are Story's, Chitty's, and Byle's elaborate and scientific treatises upon bills and notes.

This part consists of rules of evidence and general rules of law, in relation to bills of exchange, &c., together with a large number of forms useful to all classes of business men; such as bonds, receipts, &c., &c.

* * * * * * * * * *

ROCHESTER, *January*, 1851.

PREFACE

TO THE REVISED EDITION.

In the revision of this work, such alterations have been made, as were necessary, to meet more fully the wants of both teacher and pupil. These alterations are confined entirely to the arrangement of the materials of the book—so that the new edition may be used with the old, without creating confusion. In making these alterations, we have endeavored to avoid the necessity of the pupil's turning pages for references, by having examples, explanations, and memoranda, as far as possible, on opposite pages;—to increase the discipline it gives the student, by changing many of the examples from the script to the memoranda form, in order that, instead of merely copying, the pupil may be compelled to apply the principles;—to aid both teacher and pupil in the prosecution of the study, by the insertion of a large number of questions in connection with each form;—to simplify some portions of the work, as the Trial Balance, Balance Sheet, &c. These, with other changes, are such as have been suggested by those who have made practical use of the book, and have tested both its virtues and faults. It is believed that these alterations and additions, together with the new type and style of script, will add greatly to the value and efficiency of the work, thereby insuring it a warm welcome among its patrons.

Troy, 1863.

COMMERCIAL ABBREVIATIONS.

THE following is a list of the abbreviations used in this work, and those commonly used in Book-keeping:

Acct. . . . .Account.
Agt. . . . .Agent.
Amt. . . . . .Amount.
@. . . . . . . .At.
Aug. . . . . .August.

Bal. . . . . . .Balance.
Bbl. . . . . . .Barrel.
B. B. . . . . .Bill Book.
Bk. B. . . . .Bank Book.
Blk. . . . . . .Black.
Bot. . . . . . .Bought.
B. P. . . . . .Bill of Parcels.
Bro. . . . . . .Broad.
Brot. . . . . .Brought.
Bush. . . . . .Bushel.

C. B. . . . . . .Cash Book.
Co. . . . . . . .Company
Com. . . . . . .Commission.
Cr. . . . . . . .Creditor.
C. S. B. . . . Commission Sales Book.
Cts. . . . . . .Cents.
Cwt. . . . . . .Hundred Weight.
Cap. . . . . . .Capital.

Dft. . . . . . .Draft.
Disct. . . . . .Discount.
Do. or Ditto. The Same.
Doz. . . . . . Dozen.
Dr. . . . . . . .Debtor.
Ds. . . . . . . .Days.
D. B. . . . . .Day-Book.
Dec. . . . . . .December.

E. E. . . . . .Errors Excepted.
Exch. . . . . .Exchange.

Gall. . . . . . .Gallon.
Gro. . . . . . .Gross.

Hdkf. . . . . .Handkerchief.
Hhd. . . . . . .Hogshead.

I. B. . . . . . .Invoice Book.
Inst. . . . . . .Instant.
Int. . . . . . . .Interest.
i. e. . . . . . . .That is.

Ins. . . . . .Insurance.
Invt. . . . . .Inventory.

Jan. . . . . .January.
J. F. . . . . .Journal Folio.

Lab. . . . . .Labor.
Lbs . . . . .Pounds.
Led. . . . . .Ledger.

Manufg. . . . . . . .Manufacturing.
Mdse. . . . . .Merchandise.
Mos. . . . . .Months.

No. . . . . .Number.
N. B. . . . . .Take Notice.

Oz. . . . . .Ounce.

Payt. . . . . .Payment.
Pd. . . . . .Paid.
Per. . . . . .By.
Pr. . . . . .Pair.
Ps. . . . . .Pieces.
P. C. B. . . . . . . .Petty Cash Book.
P. & L. . . . . .Profit and Loss.
P. . . . . .Page.
Prem. . . . . .Premium.

Qrs. . . . . .Quarters.

Recd. . . . . .Received.
Recvble. . . . . . . .Receivable.
Rend. . . . . .Rendered.
R. R. . . . . .Railroad.

S. B. . . . . .Sales Book.
Shipt. . . . . .Shipment.
Sks. . . . . .Skeins.
Sps. . . . . .Spools.

Thd. . . . . .Thread.

Ult. . . . . .Last Month.

Viz. . . . . .Namely.

Yds. . . . . .Yards.
Yr. . . . . .Year.

Dr. Isaac H. Jameson Cr.

1848						1848				
Jan.	1	To 5 Bush. Wheat	1.25	6	25	Feb.	15	By Cash	4	00
Mar.	4	" 12 lbs. Butter	.15	1	80	May	1	" do.	5	00
"	"	" 18 " Cheese	.8	1	44	"	10	" "	3	59
"	"	" 10 Bush. Oats	.31	3	10					
				12	59				12	59

PART FIRST.

FORM FOR FARMERS.

This Form requires but one book, in which two pages opposite each other are appropriated for each individual account. The name of the person should be written in a bold hand at the top of the page, and the letters *Dr.* at the right of the name on the left-hand page, and *Cr.* at the right of the name on the right-hand page. Each page should be divided by perpendicular lines into five spaces, the first for the month, the second for the day of the month, the third for the items, the fourth and fifth for dollars and cents. Whenever you trust the person with any thing, the date, name, and value of the thing should be placed on the left-hand or debit page; and whenever he pays or trusts you with any thing, the date, name, and value in dollars and cents should be placed on the right-hand or credit page of his account.

For example, if, on the first of January, 1848, you sell I. H. Jameson five bushels of wheat at one dollar and twenty-five cents a bushel, and on the fifteenth day of February following he pays you four dollars; on the fourth day of March you sell him twelve pounds of butter at fifteen cents per pound, eighteen pounds of cheese at eight cents per pound, and ten bushels of oats at thirty-one cents per bushel; and on the first day of May he pays you cash five dollars; and on the tenth day of May, you wish to close the account, and so ask him for what he still owes you, and he pays you the amount in cash, i. e., three dollars and fifty-nine cents—the entries would be as on the opposite page.

All the accounts should be kept in the above manner, and on the first day of January, or of some other month, in each year, should be settled, and the book balanced.

In settling with a person, if he pays you in cash, or gives you his note to balance his account, give him credit accordingly, as in the account of I. H. Jameson, on the preceding page.

If you pay him cash, or give him your note to balance, charge him accordingly. If the account is not balanced by cash paid, or note given, it should be done by giving the person credit, or charging him with enough to balance it. For instance, if you find that he is owing you, give him credit for the amount "By Balance," and charge the same to him in the new account. If, on the other hand, you find that you are owing him, make him debit for the amount "To Balance," and credit him with same in the new account.

QUESTIONS.

What is this form called? How many pages are used for each account? Why should the pages be opposite? How should each account be headed? At which side of the name should the letters, *Dr.* and *Cr.*, be placed? Into how many spaces should each page be divided? For what is the first space used? the second? the third? the fourth? the fifth? Whenever you trust the person with any thing, on which page do you place it? If the person trust you, on which page? What three things must be put down in each entry? When should accounts be settled? What is meant by the terms "balance"—"balancing an account?" If the account is not balanced by cash, or a note, how do you balance it? If you credit the person with the balance, on which page of the new account do you make the entry? If you debit him, on which page?

EXAMPLES FOR PRACTICE.

Rule a sheet of paper as directed, and enter the following accounts, in the same manner as that of I. H. Jameson.

Example I.

On the first day of January, 1861, you sell Daniel White ten bushels of wheat at one dollar and ten cents a bushel—three bushels of potatoes at eighty cents a bushel—on the fourth day of February, he pays you ten dollars—on the fifth day of March he sells you two dozen eggs at eighteen cents a dozen—on the eighth day of April, you sell him six pounds of butter at twenty cents a pound—and on the first day of June, he pays you four dollars and twenty-four cents to balance the account.

Example II.

On the second day of June, 1861, you sell George Johnson, a horse for one hundred and fifty dollars—on the sixth day of June, he sells you a cow for sixty dollars—on the eighth day of June, he sells you twenty bushels of oats at forty cents a bushel—on the ninth day of June, you sell him forty pounds of wool at forty-five cents a pound—on the first day of August, he gives you his note at six months for one hundred dollars to balance the account.

INDEX.

The Index is sometimes a separate book, but it usually is placed in the front part of the Account-Book. Several pages are divided into spaces, as on the opposite page; Each space is marked by a letter. The Index is used to enable us to refer the more readily to accounts in the book. For example, we enter the account of A. I. Hovey on the first page of the book. We look in the Index for the space marked by the letter H., the initial of his name, and enter his name and the number of the page. Whenever we enter any account in the book, we enter the name and number of page, in the space of the Index marked by the initial of the name. In order to refer to any account, we turn to the Index, and the space marked with the initial of the name, and there find the page on which is the account, to which we can then at once turn. Sometimes, instead of one page being divided into spaces, each letter has a separate page. If the account should be transferred to another page, the number of the new page must, also, be placed in the Index by the name. After the learner has thoroughly studied the foregoing principles—let him prepare paper and enter the following accounts, that are explained. Let the paper be ruled with care—the writing distinct—the figures correctly made—and the balancing lines drawn perfectly straight.

INDEX TO FARMER'S FORM.

1 *Albert J. Hovey* Dr.

1848					
Jan.	3	To 8 Cords Wood	2.00	16	00
"	11	" 2 Tons Hay	7.50	15	00
Feb	4	" 10 Bush. Apples	.25	2	50
Mar.	18	" 1 " Clover Seed		5	00
Apr.	1	" 9 Doz. Eggs	.10		90
"	30	" 5 lbs. Butter	.15		75
June	28	" 8 Weeks Pasturing Cow	.25	2	00
"	"	" 6 do. do. Horse	.38	2	28
"	30	" 14 Doz. Eggs	.08	1	12
Oct.	16	" 8 lbs. Butter	.13	1	04
Dec.	31	" Cash to Balance		32	24
				78	83

The foregoing account is with a merchant. On the left-hand page he is debited with every thing you have let him have, and on the right-hand page he is credited for every thing you have purchased of him. On the 31st day of December, 1848, you wish to settle this account, which is done in the following manner.

In the first place you add the sums in the money columns of the debit side of the account, and find they amount to forty-six dollars and fifty-nine cents, which is the sum total of all that you have let him have. You next add the sums in the money columns of the credit side, and find they amount to seventy-eight dollars and eighty-three cents, which is the value of all the articles you have pur-

Albert J. Hovey Cr.[1]

1848					
Jan.	5	By 2 Yds. Broadcloth	5.00	10	00
"	"	" Trimmings for Coat		2	12
"	11	" 2 Brooms	.18		36
Feb	4	" 20 lbs Sugar	.10	2	00
"	"	" 1 " Young Hyson Tea			88
Mar.	18	" 1 " Saleratus			06
"	"	" 1 " Ginger			12
"	"	" ¼ " Cloves	.50		13
Apr.	1	" 17 Yds. Sheeting	.13	2	21
"	"	" 2 " Linen	.75	1	50
"	29	" 20 lbs. Candles	.12	2	40
May	4	" 2¾ Yds. Cassimer	2.00	5	50
"	"	" Bill of Goods for James		31	81
June	3	" 24 lbs. Sugar	.09	2	16
Sept.	14	" 2 " Tea	.75	1	50
Oct.	16	" 10 " Coffee	.12	1	20
Dec.	4	" Bill of Crockery		14	88
				78	83

chased of him. You then subtract the forty-six dollars and fifty-nine cents, the amount you have let him have, from the seventy-eight dollars and eighty-three cents, the amount purchased of him, and find the difference to be thirty-two dollars and twenty-four cents, which is the amount you owe him. You then pay him this amount, and enter it on the debit side of his account, "To Cash to Balance." The debit and credit sides will now foot alike. You next draw single lines opposite each other under these columns, and after adding and placing the amount under them, you draw double lines to signify that the two sides are balanced and closed.

James Rogers Dr

1848					
Jan.	15	To 5 Bush. Wheat	1 12	5	60
"	29	" 1 Ton Hay		8	00
Mar.	4	" 36 lbs. Ham	.07	2	52
Apr.	14	" 8 Bush. Oats	.38	3	04
"	27	" 1 Cord Wood		1	50
May	1	" 8 lbs. Butter	.15	1	20
June	30	" 5 Bush. Potatoes	.38	1	90
Aug.	16	" 6 Doz. Eggs	.10		60
Oct.	28	" 32 lbs. Cheese	.07	2	24
Dec.	20	" 1 Hide 78 lbs.	.05	3	90
				30	50
Dec.	30	To Balance		4	12

MEMORANDA OF THE ABOVE ACCOUNT

Jan. 4th, 1848. Bo't of J. Rogers, 1 pr. fine sewed boots, at $6.00. 15th. Sold him 5 bushels of wheat, at $1.12. 29th. Sold him a ton of hay, at $8.00. Feb. 12th. Bo't of him 1 pr. of stoga boots for James, at $2.50; and 2 prs. of boots for boys, $1.75 Mar. 4th. Sold him 36 lbs. of ham, at $.07. 27th. He mended boots for James, $.75. 31st. Bo't of him 1 pr. woman's boots for Julia, $1.50. April 14th. Sold him 8 bushels of oats, at $.38. 27th. Sold him 1 cord of wood, at $1.50. May 1st. Sold him 8 lbs. of butter, at $.15. June 19th. Bo't of him 1 pr. morocco shoes, at $1.25. 30th. Sold him 5 bushels of potatoes, at $.38. July 8th. He mended shoes, $1.13. 24th. Bo't of him 1 pr. gaiter boots, $2.00. Aug. 16th. Sold him 6 doz. eggs, at $.10. Oct. 9th. Bo't 1 pr. of fine boots, for James, at $4.00. 28th. Sold him 32 lbs. of cheese, at $.07. Nov. 13th. Bo't of him 1 pr. fine brogans, at $2.00. Dec. 20th. Sold him 1 hide, 78 lbs., $ 05. 25th. Bo't of him 1 pr. pumps for James, $1.75.

James Rogers — *Cr.* 2

1848					
Jan.	*4*	*By 1 Pr. Fine Sewed Boots*		*6*	*00*
Feb.	*12*	*" 1 " Stoga Boots for James*		*2*	*50*
"	*"*	*" 2 " Boots for Boys*	*1.75*	*3*	*50*
Mar.	*27*	*" Mending Boots for James*			*75*
"	*31*	*" 1 Pr. Woman's Boots for Julia*		*1*	*50*
June	*19*	*" 1 " Morocco Shoes*		*1*	*25*
July	*8*	*" Mending*		*1*	*13*
"	*24*	*" 1 Pr. Gaiter Boots*		*2*	*00*
Oct.	*9*	*" 1 " Fine Boots for James*		*4*	*00*
Nov.	*13*	*" 1 " Brogans*		*2*	*00*
Dec.	*25*	*" 1 " Pumps for James*		*1*	*75*
"	*30*	*" Balance*		*4*	*12*
				30	*50*

On comparing this memoranda, with the entries in the account above, you will find that whenever I sold J. Rogers any article, I made an entry on the debit side—as in the item, 5 bus. of wheat—placing in the first space the month—in the second, the day of the month—in the third the word "To," followed by the name of the articles, carrying out into the fourth and fifth, the total cost. On the other hand, whenever I bought any thing of him, I made the entry on the other page—observing the same order. On Dec. 30th, I wished to balance this acc't. To do this, I add up the column on the debit page, and find that it amounts to $30.50. I then add up the column on the credit page, which amounts to $26.38. I then subtract the amount of credit from the amount of the debit column, and the remainder, shows that he still owes me $4.12. I then make the entry, "Dec. 30th, By balance $4.12;" and draw the lines, which denote that the account is balanced. I then open a new account, either on a new page, or, as in this case, on the same page, and make as the first entry—"Dec. 30th. To balance $4.12." I charge him with $4.12 in the new account, because that is the amount I give him credit for, in the old account, in order to balance it.

3 **Dwight Foster** **Dr.**

1848					
Mar.	4	To 3 Yds. Gray Cloth	.75	2	25
Apr.	28	" 2 Days' Work with Team	1.50	3	00
Aug.	5	" 5 lbs. Fine Wool	.38	1	90
"	"	" Cash		25	00
Oct.	14	" 8 Bush. Apples	.25	2	00
"	26	" 1 Ton Hay		6	00
Nov.	11	" 4 Bush. Corn in the Ear	.25	1	00
"	"	" 1 Load Straw		1	00
Dec.	8	" 2 Cords Wood	2.00	4	00
"	30	" my Note at 6 months to Balance		17	10
				63	25

MEMORANDA OF ABOVE ACCOUNT.

1848. Jan. 22d. Bo't of Dwight Foster 1 brass plated harness, $30.00. Mar. 4th. Sold him 3 yds. of gray cloth, at $.75. April 28th. I worked for him 2 days, with team, at $1.50 per day. Same date. Bo't of him 1 pr. of breast straps $1, and 2 hame straps at $.25 a piece. June 8th. He repaired my harness, $2.00. Aug. 5th. I sold him 5 lbs. fine wool, $.38, and paid him $25, in cash. Aug. 19th. Bo't of him saddle, bridle and martingals, $16. Oct. 16th. Bo't of him 1 pr. of collars, $4.00, and 1 pr. of halters, $1.75. Nov. 11th. Sold him 4 bushels of corn in the ear at $.25 per bushel, and 1 load of straw, $1. Nov. 30th. Bo't of him 1 leather trunk, for James, $8.00. Dec. 8th. Sold him 2 cords of wood at $2 per cord.

Dwight Foster Cr. 3

1848					
Jan.	22	By 1 Brass Plated Single Harness		30	00
Apr.	28	" 1 Pr. Breast Straps		1	00
"	"	" 2 Hame Straps	.25		50
June	8	" Repairing Harness		2	00
Aug.	19	" Saddle, Bridle & Martingals		16	00
Oct.	16	" 1 Pr. Collars		4	00
"	"	" 1 " Halters		1	75
Nov.	30	" 1 Leather Trunk for James		8	00
				63	25

These transactions would be entered as above. Let the pupil compare, carefully, each entry in the memoranda with its corresponding one in the acc't. On the 30th December I wish to close the account. As in the preceding account of James Rogers, I first find the am't of debit column, and then of the credit column. Having subtracted the smaller from the greater, I find that I still owe him $17.10. Not having the money to pay this amount, I give him my note at 6 months, and, as that represents cash, I make the entry, "Dec. 30th, To my note at 6 mo's to balance, $17.10." I then draw in the figure columns the lines as above, and having added up the columns on each page, the amounts are now of course the same. The lines drawn under the last entry on the credit page denote that the account is balanced and closed.

Potato-field, One Acre Lot Dr.

1848					
May	1	To 1 Ds. Lab. Plowing & Harrowing		2	00
"	2	" 12 Bush. Potatoes for Seed	.37½	4	50
"	"	" 2 Ds. Lab. Planting	1.00	2	00
June	20	" 1 " do. Plowing		1	50
"	"	" 2 " do. Hoeing	1.00	2	00
July	7	" 1 " do. Plowing		1	50
Sept.	15	" Digging and Covering		5	00
1849					
Mar.	17	" 3 Ds. Lab. Marketing	2.00	6	00
"	"	" Profit on one Acre of Potatoes		88	50
				113	00

MEMORANDA OF THE ABOVE ACCOUNT.

1848. May 1st, one day's labor plowing and harrowing of potato-field, $2.00. 2d. Bo't 12 bushels of potatoes for seed, at $.37½. Same day, two days' labor planting the field, at $1. June 20th, one day's labor plowing, $1.50; also, 2 days' labor, hoeing, at $1. July 7th, one day's labor plowing, $1.50. Sept. 15th. Digging and covering potatoes, $5.00; also, sold 12 bushels of potatoes, for cash, at $.25 per bushel; also, sold 25 bushels of small potatoes at $.20 per bush. 1849. Mar. 17th. Paid for 3 days' labor, marketing, at $2 per day; also received cash for 300 bushels potatoes at $.35 per bushel.

Besides accounts with persons, the farmer finds it not only convenient but useful to keep accounts with his dif-

Potato-field, One Acre Lot Cr. 4

1848					
Sept.	15	By Cash for 12 Bush. Potatoes	.25	3	00
"	"	" 25 Bush. Small Potatoes	.20	5	00
1849					
Mar.	17	" Cash for 300 Bush. Potatoes	.35	105	00
				113	00

ferent fields and departments of labor, in order to know, accurately, the yearly gains. The above account is one kept to ascertain the profit on a potato-field for one year. It is headed "Potato-field, One Acre Lot." It is made debtor to the labor of preparing and cultivating the ground, to the cost of the seed, to digging and covering the crop, and the cost of marketing. It is credited with the receipts for the crop. By adding up the columns, as in foregoing account, and subtracting the less from the greater, we find that the receipts exceed the expenses $88.50, which is then entered on the debtor side, as "March 17th, To profit on 1 acre of potatoes $88.50," in order to balance and close the account. By pursuing this method with all his fields, the farmer may determine with accuracy the whole profit arising from the cultivation of his farm.

QUESTIONS.

What is the Index? In what part of the book is it placed? Is it ever a separate book? Describe its ruling and use. How would you enter A. J. Hovey's account in Index? How does the Index enable you to refer to an account? If an account is transferred to another page in the Leger, what entry do you make in the Index?

When the learner has become so familiar with the foregoing exercises, as to be able to enter the accounts nicely on paper ruled for the purpose, let him enter in his blank book the memoranda on the following pages. The pupil should avoid all mistakes. The teacher should insist upon the entries being made with the greatest care. A blot on the page is unpardonable. All figures should be made with great neatness. The heading of each account should be in a good bold style—the entries in a clear writing without flourishes. The ruler should be used in drawing the lines. A quill pen and red ink are the best for this purpose.

Memoranda of transactions between Barney McGuinniss and myself:

1848. Feb. 8. He cut for me 8 cords of wood, at $.38 per cord. Same day, I sold him 2 bushels of wheat, at $1.12 per bushel, and 20½ lbs. of pork, at $.08 per lb. Mar. 1st. He has sawed wood for me 3 days, ending this day, at $.75 per day. April 1st. I sold him 1 bushel of corn, $.63; also ½ bus. beans, at $1.00 per bush. April 8th. He has worked 4 days drawing manure, ending to-day, at $.75 per day. April 24th. He has worked 6 days, building wall, at $.75 per day. May 8th. I sold him a pig for $.75, and plowed his garden for $.75. May 29th. He has worked for me 2 days, hoeing corn, at $.75 per day. June 7th. I sold him 3 yds. gray cloth, at $.75 per yd., and paid him $3.00 in cash. July 24th. He has worked for me 3 days, haying, at $1 per day. Aug. 12th. He has worked for me 5 days, harvesting, at $1.50 per day. Sept. 9th. I have pastured his cow for 4 weeks, ending to-day, at $.25 per week. Oct. 9th. He has worked for me 2 days, threshing, at $.88 per day. Nov. 11th. He has husked corn for me for 2 days, at $.75 per day. Nov. 13th. I sold him 4 lbs. of butter, at $.13 per lb.

If the memoranda are properly entered the pupil will find that the account will be balanced by making this entry: "Dec. 30th. To cash to balance, $14.77," the am't I owed and paid him on that day.

Memoranda of transactions between my hired man, James Hamilton, and myself:

184[illegible] Feb. 12th. Purchased a pr. of boots for James Hamilton, at $2.50. March 27th. Paid for mending his boots $.75. April 15th. Paid him cash $5.00. May 1st. I owe him for 4 mo's' labor, closing to-day, at $9.00 per month. May 4th. Paid his bill for goods at Hovey's, $31.81. May 15th. Paid Wilder, for making a suit of clothes for James Hamilton, $8. July 3d. Paid him cash $10.00, and let him the use of horse and carriage 1 day for $1.50. July 31st. I owe him for 2 mo's' labor, ending to-day, at $10 per month. Oct. 9th. Purchased for him 1 pr. of fine boots $4, and overcoat $14. Nov. 30th. Purchased for him 1 leathern trunk, $8. Dec. 25th. Purchased for him 1 pr. of pumps, $1.75. Dec. 30th. Paid him in cash $15.69, and I owe him for labor 6 mo's, ending to-day, at $12 per month.

If the memoranda are properly entered, the account will be balanced by making the following entry: "Dec. 30th. To my note at 3 mo's to balance, $25."

Memoranda of transactions between the blacksmith, James McElvain, and myself:

1848. Jan. 8th. Bo't of him 1 lumber sleigh $28.00, and he also shod my horse for $1. Feb. 9th. He set 1 shoe, $.13. April 15th. He made 1 large clevis for me, $1. May 4th. He made 2 hoes for me, at $.50. June 8th. He sharpened Colter, $.13, and shod my horses for $1.75. Aug. 5th. He set wagon tire for me, $1; also mended chain, $.13. Aug. 14th. I sold him 1 ton of hay, $8. Sept. 9th. He ironed whippletrees for me, $1.50. Oct. 22d. I sold him 5 cords of wood, at $2 per cord. Nov. 15th. Sold him 4 bus. of wheat at $1.12 per bush.; 16 bus. of oats at $.38 per bus.; and 3 bus. of corn, at $.62 per bus. Nov. 18th. Bo't of him 14 lbs. of gate hinges at $.13. Dec. 21st. Worked for him 1 day with team, $1.50.

If the memoranda are properly entered, the account will be balanced by making the following entry: "Dec. 30th. To cash to balance, $5.54."

Memoranda of transactions between the tailor, Chester Wilder, and myself:

1848. February 1st. He made a coat for me, $5.00. March 15th. Sold him 1 cord of wood, $2.00. March 16th. He cut 2 pairs of pants for the boys at $.19 each; also, bought of him 1 satin vest, $4.00. April 8th. Sold him 6 lbs. of butter, at $.15 per lb. May 15th. He made suit of clothes for James, $8.00. June 22. Sold him 1 bbl. of flour $6.00, and paid him cash $10.50. Oct. 9th. Bo't of him an overcoat for James, $14.00. Oct. 18th. He cut 2 coats for boys, at $.38 a piece. Nov. 23d. Sold him ½ ton of hay, at $8 per ton. Dec. 11th. Sold him a hog, weighing 249 lbs., at $.4 per lb. Dec. 25th. Bought of him 1 pair of cassimere panta loons, $6.00.

If the above memoranda are properly entered, the account will be balanced by making the following entry: "Dec. 30th. To cash and balance, $4.78."

Memoranda of expenditures and receipts incurred in fattening 5 hogs, kept to ascertain the profit. (Pork account.)

1848. Oct. 15th. Bought 5 hogs, total weight 1187 lbs. a $,03 per lb.; and 75 bushels of corn at $.50 per bushel. Nov. 13th. Paid $.05 per bushel for grinding 30 bus. of corn. Dec. 16th. Paid cash $5 for butchering the pigs. Dec. 16th. Laid by 672 lbs. pork for family use at $.05 per lb. Dec. 17th. Sold 1,167 lbs. pork, at $.05 per lb.

If the above memoranda are properly entered, the account will be balanced by making the following entry: "Dec. 17. To profit on fattening pork, $12.34."

Memoranda of expenditures and receipts, in cultivating 5 acres of corn, kept to ascertain profit. (Cornfield account.)

1848. May 1. Manured 5 acres at $2 per acre. May 3d. 3 days' plowing, at $2 per day. May 4th. 1 day harrowing, $2. May 5th. 1½ days furrowing, at $1.50 per day. May 6th. ¾ bushel of seed corn, at

$1 per bl.; and 4 days' planting at $.75 per day. June 6th. Cultivated 4 days, $1.50 per day, and hoed 5 days, $.75 per day. July 8th. Plowed 3 days, $1.50 per day, and hoed 5 days, $.75 per day. Sept. 5th. 4 days cutting up the corn, $.75 per day. Nov. 1st. 16 days husking, $.75 per day, and 2 days drawing in at $2.00. Nov. 1st. Stored for home use 56 bushels ears soft corn at $.12½, and 163 bushels hard corn at $.25; also cornstalks, $10. Nov. 2d. Sold 2 loads of pumpkins at $.75 per load, and reserved 6 loads for home use at $.50 per load. Dec. 14th. 3 days threshing and cleaning corn, at $.75 per day; also 2 days marketing, at $2 per day. Dec. 14th. Sold 140 bushels shelled corn, at $.50 per bushel. Dec. 15th. Interest on 5 acres at $50, at 7 per cent.=$250×.07=$17.50.

If the above memoranda be properly entered, the account will be balanced by making the following entry: "Dec. 16th. To profit on crop, $47.50."

Memoranda of expenditures and receipts in cultivating 10 *acres of wheat kept to ascertain profit.* (*Wheatfield account.*)

1848. June 16th. Plowed 7 days at $2. June 19th. Harrowed 2 days at $2. Sept. 6th. Worked 6 days cultivating at $2; also, sowed 17½ bushels seed wheat at $1.25; also worked 1 day at sowing, at $1.00, and 2 days furrowing and ditching at $2. 1849. August 9. Harvested 10 acres at $1.50 per acre. Aug. 15th. Drew the wheat into the barn, $6. Sept. 28th. Threshed 200 bushels at .07 pr. bush. Oct. 5th. Took 15 bushels for family use at $1.00 per bl., and sold 85 bushels at $1.06. Oct. 15th. Marketed 200 bushels, a $,03 per bl. sold 100 bushels at $1.00; allowed for wear of implements, $2.00; also interest on 10 acres at $50 at 7 per cent.=$500×.07=$35.

If the above memoranda be properly entered, the account will be balanced by making the following entry: "Oct. 16th. To profit on 10 acres of wheat, $70.22."

PRACTICAL EXERCISES.

FARMER'S FORM.

THE learner having carefully studied, and practiced upon the preceding accounts, may, now, enter in his blank-book the memoranda on the following pages, being careful, to write distinctly, and to make all the letters and lines correctly, avoiding mistakes. In these memoranda the names are not given, but the occupation, as merchant, blacksmith, shoemaker, tailor, &c. The learner may substitute for these the names of persons with whom he is acquainted, following these occupations. The price per yard, ounce, pound, ton, day, month, pair, piece, &c., is given, leaving the amount to be extended by the learner. He may also substitute the abbreviations, wherever they can be, in place of the whole word.

The accounts to be opened in this set are with a merchant, shoemaker, blacksmith, tailor, harness-maker, hired man, neighbor, cornfield, and wheatfield; and if the transactions are properly disposed of, the balances will show that I am indebted as follows: To the shoemaker, $8.20; the hired man, $82.31; the harness-maker, $19.00; the blacksmith; $9.00; the merchant, $5.25. The tailor owes me $11.09; my neighbor owes me $1.25. Profit on 10 acres of corn, $85.83; do. on 15 acres of wheat, $185.08.

The foregoing principles are sufficient to enable any farmer to keep accurate accounts—ascertaining what crops, &c., are the most profitable. It is the usual custom to keep the cash account in a separate book, called the cash-book—a full explanation of that book is given in another part of this volume.

MEMORANDUM FOR 1850.

JANUARY.

5th. Sold the tailor 2 cords of wood, at $2.12½. Bought of the shoemaker 2 pair of stoga boots, at $2.50. 14th. Bought of the tailor 1 pair of pantaloons for my hired man, at $6.00. 15th. Sold the shoemaker 3 cords of maple wood, at $2.00, and bought of him 1 pair of woman's boots, at $1.50. 19th. The tailor has cut a pair of pantaloons for me, at 25c., and a coat at 50c. 28th. Sold the harness-maker 1 ton of hay at $8.00, and bought of him 1 single harness at $20.00.

FEBRUARY.

9th. Drew wood for my neighbor to-day with my team, at $1.50. 16th. Bought of the shoemaker 2 pair of children's shoes, at 75c., and had a pair mended, at 25c. 20th. Paid my hired man, cash, $5.00. 23d. Sold the shoemaker half a ton of hay, at $7.00, and half a bushel of beans, at $1.00. 25th. My hired man has lost 2 days time, at 50c. 28th. The tailor has made a vest for me, at $1.50.

MARCH.

9th. Worked for the blacksmith 1½ days with my team, at $1.50. 16th. The blacksmith mended my hay-knife, at 25c. Bought of the merchant 30 yards of Brown Factory, at 10c., and half a dozen spools of white thread, at 62c. 23d. Bought 1 lb. Young Hyson tea, at 75c., and sold him 1½ tons of hay, at $8.00. 25th. Sold the harness-maker 25 bundles of rye straw, at 4c., and he has repaired my harness, at $4.00.

APRIL.

6th. Sold the blacksmith 9 pounds of butter, at 14c. 15th. My neighbor has plowed for me 1 day with his team, at $1.50. The blacksmith has ironed my whippletrees, at $1.25, and sharpened my colter, at 12c. 18th. Sold the blacksmith 5 bushels of potatoes, at 50. 23d. The shoemaker has tapped my boots, at 50c.

MAY.

1st. Bought of the blacksmith 1 large clevice, at $1.13, and plowed the shoemaker's garden, at $1.00. 4th. Finished plowing cornfield to-day, 7 days, with team, at $2.00. 5th. Planted corn 1 day for my neighbor, at 75c. 7th. Sold the tailor 4 bushels of potatoes, at 31c., and 5 lbs. of butter, at 12½c. Labored 2 days harrowing cornfield, at $2.00, and 2 days furrowing cornfield, at $1.50. 8th. Planted in cornfield 2 bushels of seed corn, at $1, and finished planting cornfield, eight days, at $1.00. 14th. My neighbor let me have 25 bushels of potatoes, at 30c. 15th.

Bought of the merchant three yards of black cassimere, at $1.50, 25 pounds of sugar, at 9c., one pound of Young Hyson tea, at 75c.; and sold him fifteen pounds of butter, at 12½c., and 9 dozen of eggs, at 10c. 31st. Bought of the harness-maker one saddle, at $14.00, and paid him cash $10.00.

JUNE.

1st. Bought of the shoemaker 2 pair of Morocco buskins, at $1.25. 6th. My neighbor has hoed corn for me, 3 days, at 75c. 8th. Cultivated cornfield eight days, with horse, at $1.50, and finished hoeing cornfield, twelve days, at $1.00. 9th. Blacksmith has repaired my wagon, at $3.25, and shod two horses, at $1.00. 15. Bought of the shoemaker 1 pair of gaiter boots, at $2.25. 21st. Sold the blacksmith 12 pounds of butter, at 12½c. 22d. Finished plowing wheatfield, fifteen acres, ten days, at $2.00. 25th. Sold the merchant 15 bushels of oats, at 30c., and gave my hired man an order on him for goods, $18.50. 26th. Finished harrowing wheatfield, three days, at $2.00.

JULY.

1st. Sold the merchant 8 pounds of butter, at 12½c., and bought of him 1 pound of Young Hyson tea, at 75c., 2 gallons of molasses, at 44c., and ten yards of calico, at 12½c. 2d. Bought of the shoemaker one pair of fine boots, for my hired man, at $4.50. 4th. Paid my hired man, cash, on account, $10.00. 5th. Finished plowing cornfield, five days, at $1.50. 15th. Bought of the blacksmith one hay-rake, at $8, and he has mended my pitchfork, at 13c. 24th. Drew hay, with team for my neighbor, one day, at $1.50. 25th. Sold the blacksmith half ton of hay, at $5.00. 31st. Sold the blacksmith one ton of hay, at $6.00.

AUGUST.

3d. The blacksmith has set my wagon tire, at $1.25, and made a linchpin, at 13c. Sold the merchant two tons of hay, at $6.00. 24th. Paid the shoemaker cash, on account, $5.00, and sold him a calf-skin weighing 10½ pounds, at 10c.

SEPTEMBER.

2d. Bought of the blacksmith one pair of small clevice,

at $1.25, and he has set one shoe, at 12c. 4th. Bought of the merchant 15 pounds of nails, at 6c., and sold him four bushels of apples, at 25c., and five pounds of butter, at 14c. 5th. Sold my neighbor eight bushels of seed wheat, at $1.25. 14th. Finished cutting up corn in cornfield, nine days, at $1.00. Labored with team on wheatfield, cultivating, ten days, at $2.00. Sowed 26 bushels of seed wheat, at $1.25. Labor, furrowing, and ditching, $5.00. Two days' labor, sowing, at $1.00. 18th. Sold the blacksmith one cord of wood, at $2.00.

OCTOBER.

5th. Sold the merchant 12 bushels of corn, at 50c., and bought of him a bill of goods amounting to $15.94. The blacksmith has ironed a lumber wagon for me, at $22.00, and made a neck yoke, at $1.25. My neighbor has threshed for me two days, at 75c. Pastured the shoemaker's cow six weeks, at 25c., and bought of him two pair of boys' boots, at $2.00. 12th. Sold my hired man 2¾ yards of gray cloth, at 75c. 17th. Threshed for my neighbor two days, at 75c. 18th. Sold the tailor 36 pounds of pork, at 8c. 19th. The tailor has made a pair of pantaloons for my hired man, at $1.00.

NOVEMBER.

2d. Measured out of the products of my cornfield, for home use, 74 bushels of ears of soft corn, at 13c.; 315 bushels of ears of sound corn, at 25c.; cornstalks, $25.00; pumpkins, at $5.00. 8th. Sold the blacksmith two bushels of turnips, at 25c. 9th. Labored in cornfield, husking, forty days, at $1.00; five days with team, drawing in, at $2.00. 13th. Bought of the merchant 1 umbrella, at $1.50, 5 pounds of coffee, at 14c., and 10 pounds of cotton batting, at 10c.; and sold him 15 bushels of potatoes, at 25c., and 20 bushels ears of corn, from cornfield, at 25c. 15th. Bought of neighbor one barrel of salt, at $1.25. 22d. The blacksmith has shod for me one pair of horses, at $2.00. Sold the tailor half a ton of hay, at $8.00. 25th. Sold the blacksmith 12 bushels of ears of corn, from cornfield, at 25c. 29th. Sold the tailor three bushels of wheat, at $1.25. Paid my hired nan, cash, $8.00. Bought of the shoemaker one pair of fine boots, at $4.50.

DECEMBER.

2d. Sold the blacksmith five barrels of cider, at $1.25. 5th. Bought of blacksmith 28 pounds of gate hinges, at 12c. 7th. Sold the shoemaker one cord of wood, at $2.25. 11th. Sold the tailor 6 yards of gray cloth, at 56c., and 14 pounds of lard, at 7c. 14th. Labored threshing corn, from cornfield, seven days, at $1.00. 16th. Received cash, for one hundred bushels of corn, at 50c. 18th. Bought of the merchant 2½ yards of cassimere, for my hired man, at $1.25, and 8 pounds of crushed sugar for myself, at 13c. Sold him two cords of body maple wood, at $2.50. The blacksmith has sharpened and set 6 shoes on my horses, at 12½c. The tailor has cut for me 2 pair of pantaloons, at 25c., and one vest at 25c. Bought of the shoemaker one pair of stoga boots, for my hired man, at $2.50. Sold the blacksmith 4 cords of wood, at $2.25, and 8 bushels of oats, at 31c. 25th. Bought of the merchant 2 gallons of molasses, at 44c., 5 pounds of raisins, at 13c., and 5 pounds of rice, at 6c. 30th. Received cash for 80 bushels of corn, at 56c. 31st. Received cash for 52 bushels of corn, at 56c. Marketing 232 bushels of corn, at 3c. My hired man has worked for me 8 months at $13.00, and 4 months at $10.00. Int. on cornfield land, 10 acres, at $50.00 per acre, at 7 per cent.

To close the account with wheatfield, it will be necessary to trespass a little on the year 1851.

August 13th. Harvesting 15 acres, at $1.25. 24th. Drawing it into the barn, $10.00. October 19th, Threshing 346 bushels of wheat, at 7c. Reserved 46 bushels for home use, at $1.00 26th. Sold, for cash, 85 bushels of wheat, at $1.25. November 15th. Sold for cash, 100 bushels of wheat, at $1.13. 18th. Sold, for cash, 80 bushels of wheat, at $1.06. 22d. Sold, for cash, 35 bushels of wheat, at $1.00. Marketing 300 bushels of wheat, at 3c. Interest on 15 acres of land, at $50.00 per acre, at 7 per cent.

FORM FOR MECHANICS.

The books necessary in this form are the Day-book and Ledger. The cash account may be kept in a separate book—forming a Cash-book, or not, at the option of the Book-keeper.

The accounts might be kept as in the Farmer's form, in one book, i. e., the Ledger; only, it would not be as convenient, for the mechanic is constantly called away from his business to attend to the wants of his customers. And, besides, having many more accounts and entries to make, than the Farmer, these accounts are of a different nature, such as cannot be remembered till evening, as those of the Farmer. Hence it is necessary, that the mechanic should use a book, in which he can make a full record of the transactions as they occur, and then at his leisure, he can arrange the various entries in their respective accounts in the Ledger.

The Day-book is a book in which all business transactions should be recorded at the time and in the order in which they occur. It is divided by perpendicular lines into seven spaces. The month occupies the first space; the day of the month, the second; the name of the person and the transaction, the third; the value of the items, in dollars and cents, the fourth and fifth; and their sum total, the sixth and seventh.

If, for example, on the first day of January, 1848, you sell Benjamin Hamilton the following articles:—One brass plated single harness for thirty dollars, one pair of halters for one dollar and seventy-five cents, and one riding bridle for one dollar and fifty cents—your Day-book entry would be as follows :

Lyons, January 1st, 1848.

Jan	*1*	*Benjamin Hamilton Dr.*				
		To 1 Brass P. S. Harness	*30*	*00*		
		" 1 Pr. Halters	*1*	*75*		
		" 1 Riding Bridle	*1*	*50*	*33*	*25*

If you had purchased the same articles of Hamilton, all the difference in the entries would have been this : after the name on the first line, in the place of *Dr.* you should have written *Cr.;* and on the next line, in the place of *To* you should have written *By.*

Whenever it is necessary to repeat the date, or the word *To* or *By*, it may be done by placing two dots (thus, ") under the date or word to be repeated. One line should be left between every two entries.

QUESTIONS.

What is this form ? How many books are needed in this form ? Name them. Is a cash book needed ? Could the accounts be kept in one book ? Why, then, do they use two ? What is the Day-book for ? When and how should the transactions be entered ? Into how many spaces is the book divided ? For what is the first space used ? the second, third, fourth, fifth, sixth, seventh ? Explain the example given ? What difference would have occurred in the entries, if you had purchased the articles of him ? Instead of repeating date, what may you write ? Instead of repeating the words *To* and *By*, what may you write ? How much space should you leave between each entry ?

DAY-BOOK.

MECHANICS' FORM.

Lyons, Saturday, January 1st, 1848.

Month	Day	Account					
Jan.	1	Isaac H. Jameson Dr.					
		To 1 Set Double Harness	26	00			
		" 1 Pr. Halters	1	75	27	75	
"	3	Henry B. Holbrook Dr.					
		To 1 S. P. Sing. Harness			35	00	
"	4	Daniel Wm. Potter Dr.					
		To 1 Pr. Breast Straps	1	00			
		" 2 " Hame do. .25		50	1	50	
"	6	Charles D. Campbell Dr.					
		To 1 Pr. Collars			3	50	
"	"	Franklin S. Clark Dr.					
		To 4 Bridles 1.25	5	00			
		" 1 Pr. Martingals		75			
		" 1 Halter		88	6	63	
"	7	Sylvester N. Nurse Dr.					
		To 1 Set S. Tug Harness	16	00			
		" 1 Breast Collar	1	75	17	75	
"	"	Bela Dunbar Dr.					
		To 1 Saddle			15	00	
"	8	Charles Harford Dr.					
		To 1 B. P. Single Harness			30	00	
"	10	James S. Hawkins Dr.					
		To 1 Set S. Tug Harness	16	00			
		" 2 Pr. Collars, 3.50	7	00			
		" 1 " Halters	1	75			
		" 1 " Tugs	3	25	28	00	

Let the pupil rule some paper and enter the following memoranda, according to directions; when he has become proficient in making the entries, he may enter them in his day-book.

MEMORANDA.

Lyons, 1848, Saturday, Jan. 1st. Sold Isaac H. Jameson 1 Set of Double Harness, $26.00, and 1 pair of Halters, $1.75. 3d. Sold Henry B. Holbrook 1 Silver plated Single Harness $35. 4th. Sold Daniel W. Potter, 1 pair of Breast Straps $1, and 2 Hame Straps, at 25c. 5th. Charles D. Campbell, 1 pair of Collars, $3.50. Also, Sold Franklin S. Clark, 4 Bridles, at $1.25, 1 pair of Martingals, $75, and 1 Halter, $88. 7th. Sold Sylvester N. Nurse, 1 Set of Single Tug Harness, $16, and 1 Breast Collar, $1.75, also sold Bela Dunbar, 1 saddle $15. 8th. Sold Charles Harford 1 Brass Plated Single Harness, $30. 10th. Sold James S. Hawkins, 1 Set Single Tug Harness, $16, 2 pair of Collars, at $3.50, 1 pair of Halters, $1.75, and 1 pair of Tugs, $3.25.

The pupil will please notice, carefully, each abbreviation, and the position of each entry on the opposite page. The entries should be so made, that if a straight line should be drawn down the page it would pass thro' the initial of each name, another thro' the word "To," another thro' the word, "Dr." Attention to these particulars will insure that neatness and precision, which are absolutely necessary in book-keeping.

Lyons, Wednesday, Jan. 12th, 1848.[2]

Month	Day	Account					
Jan.	12	Clark N. Fulton Dr.					
		To 1 Set B. Pl. Harness		38	00		
		" 1 Pr. Breast Collars		5	50		
		" 1 " Martingals			75	44	25
"	13	Aaron B. Patterson Dr.					
		To 1 Single Harness				22	00
"	"	Isaac H. Jameson Dr.					
		To 1 Halter Strap			31		
		" Mending Tug			13		44
"	15	Cornelius O. Rumsey Dr.					
		To 1 Pr. Collars		3	00		
		" 1 " Breast Straps		1	00	4	00
"	17	Horatio N. Short Dr.					
		To 1 Valise		3	00		
		" 1 Bridle		1	13	4	13
"	19	Henry Woodward Dr.					
		To 1 Pr. Blind Bridles		4	00		
		" 3 Hame Straps	.13		39		
		" 1 Throat Latch			12	4	51
"	"	John Lynd Dr.					
		To 1 Single Harness				18	00
"	21	Hiram Hawley Dr.					
		To Repairing Harness				3	75
	"	Andrew C. Mynderse Dr.					
		To 1 Trunk				4	50

MEMORANDA.

1848. Jan. 12th. Sold Clark N. Fulton 1 set brass plated harness, $38; 1 pair breast collars, $5.50; also 1 pair martingals, $.75. 13th. Sold Aaron B. Patterson 1 single harness, $22; also sold I. H. Jameson 1 halter strap, $.31, and mended tug, $.13. 15th. Sold Cornelius O. Rumsey 1 pair collars, $3, and 1 pair breast straps, $1. 17th. Sold Horatio N. Short 1 valise, $3, and 1 bridle, $1.13. 19th. Sold Henry Woodward 1 pair blind bridles, $4; 3 hame straps at $.13, and 1 throat latch, $.12; also, sold John Lynd 1 single harness, $18. 21st. Repaired harness for Hiram Hawley, $3.75, and sold Andrew C. Mynderse 1 trunk, $4.50.

(The above to be entered in Day-Book.)

Let the pupil study carefully these memoranda, as entered on opposite page. The date is set down first, the month in the first space, the day of the month in the second. The name of the person is placed on the same line in the third space, and in the same space near the double line the word "Dr.," if he has purchased of you, "Cr." if you have purchased of him. In the same space under the name place the word "To," if "Dr." is written after the name, and "By," if "Cr." After this word place the item, the price of each article if composed of several, as in H. Woodward's acc't—"3 Hame Straps .13"—then place amount of item, if there is one entry, in the sixth and seventh spaces, as in entry of Aaron B. Patterson. If there is more than one item, place the amount in fourth and fifth spaces, as in the account of Horatio N. Short, "To 1 Valise 3.00," and then place the combined amount of the several items in sixth and seventh spaces on the same line of last item, as in H. N. Short's account, last line—

"	" 1 Bridle	1	13	4	13

From the preceding explanations the pupil will be able to enter the following memoranda in his Day-Book. Let them be entered in immediate connection with the memoranda on preceding pages, of which they are a continuation. Let the teacher, in examining the entries made by the pupil, notice every mistake, either in entering the memoranda, or in writing, or in figures. He should insist upon the columns of figures being so placed that figures of the same order shall come under each other.

MEMORANDA.

1848. Jan. 25th. Cleaned harness for Henry B. Holbrook, $2.50. Repaired it, $1.88. Sold him 1 halter, $.87. Also, sold Timothy N. Foster set silver-plated harness, $42; saddle and bridle, $23; and pair halters, $1.50. 26th. Repaired harness for Sylvester N. Nurse, $2.38; also covered the dash of his buggy, $3.50. Same day bought of Franklin S. Clark 1 wash-tub, $1.13, and 3 patent pails, at $.31. Also, sold Timothy G. Baldwin 1 set long tug harness, $26.00. Aaron B. Patterson has paid me cash on account, $10.00. 29th. Bought of Daniel W. Potter 19 lbs. veal, at $.04. 31st. Sold Charles D. Campbell 1 brass plated single harness, $30. Also, sold Wm. Gridley 1 pair martingals, $.75, 3 hame straps, at $.13, and 1 bum strap, $.30. Also, repaired harness for J. H. Jameson, $1, and sold him 1 pair tugs, $3, and 1 pr. tugs, $2. Also sold James S. Hawkins 1 brass plated gig harness, $20, and repaired harness, $2.75. Also sold James H. Gillett 1 saddle, $18, 1 bridle, $1.50, 1 pair martingals, $1, and 1 halter, $1. February 1st. Sold Henry Woodward 1 pair fine boots for self, $4. Also, Bela Dunbar 1 pair boots for hired man, $2.50, and 1 pair buskins for wife, $1.25. Also, sold Aaron B. Patterson 1 pair kip boots for George, $3.25, and repaired boy's boots, $.13. 3d. Sold Hiram Hawley 1 pair shoes, $1.50, 1 pair children's shoes, $.75, and 1 pair small children's shoes, $.50. 4th. Footed fine boots for Timothy N. Foster, $3. Also tapped and patched boots for Sylvester N. Nurse, $.50, mended shoes, $.13, and sold him pair of shoes for wife, $1.50. 5th. Sold Charles Harford 2 pair small shoes, at $.50. Also mended boots for Andrew C. Mynderse, $.38. 7th. Bought of Timothy G. Baldwin 12 lbs. butter, $.13. 10th. Sold Clark N. Fulton 1 pair gaiter boots, $2. 11th. Sold Henry B. Holbrook 1 pair fine boots, $5.50, and 1 pair boy's ditto, $1.75. 14th. Sold Horace O. Bigelow 1 pair buskins for wife, $1.25. 15th. Sold

William Gridley 1 pair stoga boots, $2.50, and 1 pair women's shoes, $1.00. 17th. Sold Cornelius O. Rumsey 2 pair stoga boots, at $2.50. 18th. Bought of Horatio N. Short 1 bbl. of flour, $7. Also sold Franklin S. Clark 1 pair pumps, $1.75. 21st. Sold John Lynd 3 pair buskins, at $1.25 22d. Sold James S. Hawkins 6 pairs stoga boots at $2.50. 25th. Sold Daniel W Potter 1 pair fine boots for Eddy, $5.50. Same day, bought of him 27 lbs. pork, at $.09. 26th. Charles Harford has paid me cash $25. 28th. Isaac H. Jameson 1 pair gaiters for wife, $2, and footed fine boots, $3.50. 29th. Sold Henry Woodward 1 pair prunell shoes, $1.50, 1 pair small shoes, $.75, and mended shoes, $.38. March 1st. Shod horses for Daniel W. Potter, $2.00. 2d. Sold William Gridley 13 lbs. gate hinges, at $.13, and 4 lbs. bolts, at $.14. Same day, sold Sylvester N. Nurse 3 linch pins, $.12, repaired wagon for him, $.50, set wagon tire, $.50, and ironed neck yoke, $1.00. 3d. Mended chain for Henry B. Holbrook, $.13, and sharpened 2 shoes, $.31. Also sharpened colter for Horatio N. Short, $.13. Also sold James S. Hawkins 1 large clevis, $1.13, 1 pair small clevises, $1.25, and ironed whippletrees, $3. 4th. Shod horse for Andrew C. Mynderse, $1. 6th. Sold Charles Harford 1 linch pin, $.12, 1 hook and staple, $.13, mended shovel, $.13, and set 2 shoes, $.31. 8th. Repaired wagon for Woodward, $3. 9th. Mended log chain for Bela Dunbar, $.19, and shod his horse, $1.00. 10th. Sold Isaac H. Jameson 17 lbs. gate hinges, at $.13, and shod his horse, $1. 13th. Repaired sulkey for John Lynd, $3.50. Also bought of Henry Woodward 19 lbs. pork, at $.07, 21 lbs. pork, at $.06, and 3 bushels wheat, at $1.50. 14th. Sold Hiram Hawley 1 large clevis, $1.25, and sharpened drag teeth, $.93. Also shod horses for Timothy N. Foster, $2. 15th. Shod horse for Franklin S. Clark, toed and set 2 shoes, $.31, and set 2 new shoes, $.50. 17th. Sold Clark N. Fulton 3 bolts, at $.13, 2 linch pins, at $.12. 18th. Set 1 tire for Timothy G. Baldwin, $.38, and mended skein on wagon, $.50. Also sold Daniel W. Potter 1 hook to trace chain, $.13. 20th. Sold Charles D. Campbell 1 king bolt, $.75. 21st. Bought of Hiram Hawley 5 tons of hay, at $8. 22d. Sold Horace O. Bigelow 2 bands for drag, $.38, mended chain, $.12, and shod horses, $2. 23d. Henry B. Holbrook has paid me cash, $15. Sold Henry Woodward 1 hook and staple, $.13. Also shod horses for James H. Gillett, $2. 24th. Sold Cornelius O. Rumsey 1 iron wedge, $.88, 1 linch pin, $.12, and shod horse, $1. Also repaired drag for Timothy G. Baldwin, $.75. 27th. Bought of Daniel W. Potter 8 dozen eggs, $.10. Also repaired threshing machine for Isaac H. Jameson, $4.75. 29th. Repaired wagon for Sylvester N. Nurse, $2.50, and ironed neck yoke, $.88. 30th. Sold William Gridley

8 lbs. spikes, at $.12½, and repaired cart, $1.88. 31st. Bought of Cornelius O. Rumsey 12 lbs. butter, at $.13, 8 lbs. butter, at $.10, 22 lbs. pork, at $.07, 23 lbs. pork, at $.06, and he has paid me cash, $5. Henry B. Holbrook has paid me cash to balance his account, $32.94. Daniel W. Potter has paid me cash to balance acc't, $5.14. Charles D. Campbell has paid me cash to balance acc't, $34.25. Franklin S. Clark has given me his note at 6 months, $7.13, to balance acc't.

Entry should be—

"Franklin S. Clark Cr.
By note at 6 mo's to bal. acc't, $7.13."

Sylvester N. Nurse has given me his note, at 3 mo's for $31.50, to balance acc't. William Gridley has paid me cash to balance acc't, $10.07. Bela Dunbar has paid me cash, $19.94. Charles Harford has given me his note at 30 days for $6.69. Henry Woodward has paid me cash, $7.18. Timothy G. Baldwin has paid me cash, $26.07. James S. Hawkins has given me his note at 6 mo's for $71.13. I have allowed and credited John Lynd his acc't against me, $18.75.

Entry should be—

John Lynd Cr.
By am't of his acc't, $18.75.

I have allowed and credited Isaac H. Jameson his acc't against me, $13.75, and he has given me his note at 3 mo's to balance account, $33.90.

INDEX AND LEDGER.

MECHANICS' FORM.

A

B

Baldwin, Timothy G.
Bigelow, Horace O.

C

Campbell, Chas. D.
Clark. Franklin S

D

Dunbar, Bela

E

F

Fulton, Clark N.
Foster, Timothy N.

G

Gridley, William
Gillet, James H.

H

Holbrook, Henry B.
Harford, Charles
Hawkins, James S.
Hawley, Hiram

J

Jameson, Isaac H.

K

L

Lynd, John

M

Mynderse, Andrew C.

N	T
Nurse, Sylvester N.	
O	**V**
P	**W**
Potter, Daniel W.	*Woodward, Henry*
Patterson, Aaron B.	
Q	**X**
R	**Y**
Rumsey, Cornelius O.	
S	**Z**
Short, Horatio N.	

ALPHABET, OR INDEX.

THE ALPHABET, or INDEX, is a small book in which are arranged, in alphabetical order, the names of all persons having accounts in the Ledger, together with the pages on which such accounts are entered.

This book was fully explained in the last set, but to assist the pupil the names of the accounts in this set have been placed in the proper places. The pupil may copy these names into the blank index. The number of the page has been purposely omitted. Let the pupil, as soon as he opens an account in the Ledger, place the number of the page opposite the name in the Index.

THE LEDGER.

The LEDGER is a book to which each person's account is transferred from the Day-book, and arranged on a page by itself. The name of such person should be written in a bold hand at the top of the page, with *Dr.* on the left and *Cr.* on the right.

Each page of the Ledger should be divided by a double perpendicular line into two equal parts; the one for the debtor, and the other for the creditor side of the account. Each of these parts should also be divided by perpendicular lines into six spaces; the first space for the month, the second for the day of the month, the third for the items, the fourth for the page of the Day-book on which the original entries were made, and the fifth and sixth for dollars and cents.

The first account to be opened in the Ledger is that of the person whose name stands first in the Day-book. As soon as it is opened it should be entered in the Alphabet.

POSTING BOOKS in this form is collecting and transferring each person's account from the Day-book to its appropriate page in the Ledger. The entries recorded in the Day-book should be posted in the order in which they occur; that is, the first entry should be the first posted, and the second entry next, and so on until they are all posted.

Whenever there is more than one article charged or credited to an individual on the same page of the Day-book, the several sums should be added, and the amount entered in the Ledger, *To*, or *By Sundries;* but when there is but one article so charged or credited, it may be specified in the Ledger.

QUESTIONS.

What is the Alphabet? What entries are made in it? For what purpose is it used? When do you make an entry in this book? What is the Ledger? How are the accounts arranged in it? How should the page in the Ledger be headed? Into how many equal parts is the Ledger page divided? What are these for? Into how many spaces should each of the parts be divided? For what are the different spaces used? Whose account must be opened first in the Ledger? What entry to be made in the Index when an account is opened in the Ledger? What is meant by "Posting Books?" How should entries in Day-book be posted? When there is more than one item in the charge on Day-book, what must be done? How will you enter the amount in Ledger? If there is but one item in the charge, what may be done?

Dr. Isaac H. Jameson Cr.

				$	cts					$	cts
1848						1848					
Jan.	1	To Sundries	1	27	75	Mar.	31	By Amt. of his Account	10	13	75
"	13	" do.	2		44	"	"	" Note to Balance	"	33	90
"	31	" do.	4	6	00						
Feb.	28	" do.	6	5	50						
Mar.	10	" do.	8	3	21						
"	27	" Repairing Machine	9	4	75						
				47	65					47	65

The pupil will find on the opposite page the account of Isaac H. Jameson, as it would appear in the Ledger.

On the first page of the Day-book you will find the name of Isaac H. Jameson, the first recorded. He is there, on the first day of January, 1848, made debtor for one set of double harness at twenty-six dollars, and one pair of halters at one dollar and seventy-five cents, the sum total is twenty-seven dollars seventy-five cents; hence, we make the entry—

Jan.	1.	To Sundries	1	$27	75

On the second page, 13th day of January, for one halter strap at thirty-one cents, and mending tug thirteen cents, sum total forty-four cents, and we make the entry next to the one just entered. On the fourth page, 31st day of January, for repairing harness one dollar, one pair of tugs three dollars, one pair of tugs two dollars, sum total six dollars. Of this we make the third entry on debit side of account. On the sixth page, 28th day of January, for footing fine boots three dollars fifty cents, one pair of gaiters for wife two dollars, sum total five dollars fifty cents, which makes the fourth entry on debit side. On the eighth page, 10th day of March, for seventeen pounds of gate hinges, at thirteen cents per pound, two dollars twenty-one cents, shoeing horse one dollar, sum total three dollars twenty-one cents. This is posted as the fifth entry on the debit side. On the ninth page, 27th day of March, for repairing threshing-machine four dollars seventy-five cents, which is entered as last entry on debit side; and on the tenth page, 31st day of March, he is made credit for the amount of his account thirteen dollars seventy-five cents, and his note to balance the account thirty-three dollars and ninety cents, and should be posted as on the following page on the credit side of the account. The same method is pursued in posting the other accounts.

(The Same Posted by Figures.)

Dr. Isaac H. Jameson Cr.

1848					1848				
Jan.	1	1,27.75. 2,.44. 4,6.00	34	19	Mar.	31	By Amt. of his Account	13	75
Feb.	28	6,5.50. 8,3.21. 9,4.75	13	46	"	"	" Note to Balance	33	90
			47	65				47	65

On the opposite page you will find the same account (Isaac H. Jameson's) posted by figures, the small figures indicating the Day-book page, and the large ones the amount of the entry transferred. When the line is filled, these sums are added, and the sum total extended into the money columns. This method is very simple, and needs no further explanation after the instructions given on preceding page. It is not as full as the first method of posting, but is adopted by some, because it occupies so much less space in the Ledger than the former. The learner, if he chooses, may practise both.

By a careful study of the account given above, and the explanations accompanying it, the pupil will be enabled readily to post the remaining accounts. In order to guide the pupil in this labor, the accounts of Henry B. Holbrook, Daniel W. Potter, Charles D. Campbell, and Franklin S. Clark are given, as they will appear, if correctly posted. If the remaining accounts are properly posted by the pupil, he will find the following amounts necessary in order to balance them: Sylvester N. Nurse, —; Horace O. Bigelow, $3.75; William Gridley, —; Bela Dunbar, —; Charles Harford, —; James S. Hawkins, —; Clark N. Fulton, $46.88; Aaron B. Patterson, $15.38; Cornelius O. Rumsey, $0.72; Horatio N. Short (Cr.), $2.74; Henry Woodward, —; John Lynd, $6.50; Hiram Hawley (Cr.), $31.32; Andrew C. Mynderse, $5.88; Timothy N. Foster, $71.50; Timothy G. Baldwin, —; James H. Gillet, $23.50.

NOTE.—The dash indicates that the accounts, after which it is placed, balance.

2 Dr. **Henry B. Holbrook** Cr.

1848				$	¢	1848				$	¢
Jan.	3	To 1 S. P. S. Harness	1	35	00	Mar.	23	By Cash	9	15	00
"	25	" Sundries	3	5	25		31	" do. to Bal.	10	32	94
Feb.	11	" do.	5	7	25						
Mar.	3	" do.	7		44						
				47	94					47	94

Dr. **Daniel W. Potter** Cr.

1848				$	¢	1848				$	¢
Jan	4	To Sundries	1	1	50	Jan.	26	By 19 lbs. Veal	3		76
Feb.	25	" 1 Pr. F. Boots	6	5	50	Feb.	25	" 27 " Pork	6	2	43
Mar.	1	" Shoeing Horses	6	2	00	Mar.	27	" 8 Doz. Eggs	9		80
"	18	" 1 Hook to Chain	8		13	"	31	" Cash to Bal.	10	5	14
				9	13					9	13

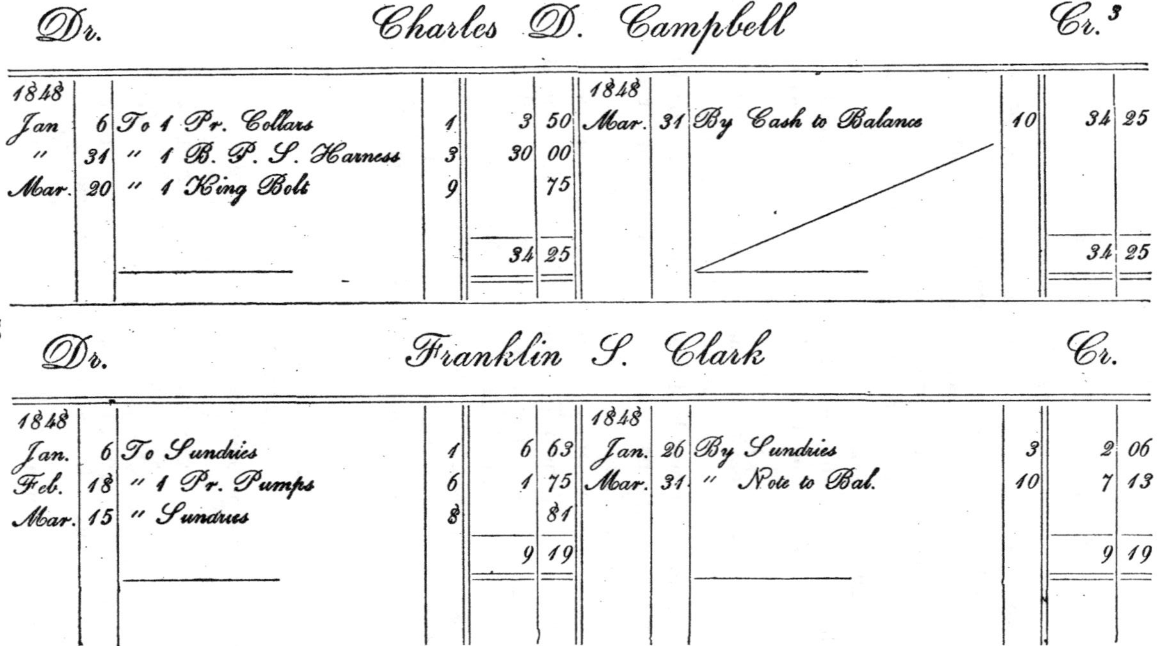

Dr. **Charles D. Campbell** Cr. 3

				$	cts					$	cts
1848						1848					
Jan	6	To 1 Pr. Collars	1	3	50	Mar.	31	By Cash to Balance	10	34	25
"	31	" 1 B. P. S. Harness	3	30	00						
Mar.	20	" 1 King Bolt	9		75						
				34	25					34	25

Dr. **Franklin S. Clark** Cr.

				$	cts					$	cts
1848						1848					
Jan.	6	To Sundries	1	6	63	Jan.	26	By Sundries	3	2	06
Feb.	18	" 1 Pr. Pumps	6	1	75	Mar.	31	" Note to Bal.	10	7	13
Mar.	15	" Sundries	8		81						
				9	19					9	19

PRACTICAL EXERCISES.

The form on the preceding pages, although it is designated as the "Mechanic's Form," is, nevertheless, well adapted to the use of professional men and merchants ; and from the fact that a majority of merchants, in the small villages throughout the country, keep their books after this form, we have thought best to give a Memorandum of the business transactions of a merchant for three months, requiring the pupil to record them in the Day-Book, post to the Ledger, and balance the accounts as in the preceding. The price per ounce, pound, gallon, yard or piece, is given, leaving the amount to be extended by the learner ; and if the above-described operation is correctly performed, it will be found, on balancing the books, that the following persons are indebted to you for the sums opposite each name :—Hiram Mann, $39.42 ; Milton Seely, $42.71 ; Albert J. Hovey, $7.17 ; Charles R. Hecox, $4.49 ; William F. Ashley, $9.15 ; Ephraim B. Price, $6.43 ; Peter Brant, $17.63 ; William Walling, $7.52 ; Merrit Thornton, $23.03 ; John Messenger, $1.71 ; Alpheus Clark, $8.81 ; Samuel Weaver, $28.66 ; John Hancock, $12.63 ; Samuel Moore, $17.21 ; Nathan Brittan, $5.36 ; and you are indebted to Myron Holmes, $2.32.

MEMORANDUM.

JANUARY

1st. Sold Hiram Mann $2\frac{1}{2}$ yds. broadcloth, at $3.00, $1\frac{1}{4}$ yd. silk serge, at $1.50, 1 doz. large buttons, at 75c., and $\frac{1}{2}$ doz. small, do., at 25c. 2d. Sold Myron Holmes 10 yds. silk, at $1.50, and 5 skeins silk, at 4c.; Milton Seely, 1 cap for boy, at $1.25, and 1 pair small coarse boots, at $1.50 ; Albert J. Hovey, 10 lbs. sugar, at 10c., and 1 lb. tea, at $1.00. 3d. Sold Charles R. Hecox 5 yds. calico, at 10c., 5 lbs. coffee, at 14c., and 1 lb. tea, at $1.00 ; William F. Ashley, 15 lbs. sugar, at 10c., 1 oz. nutmegs, at 12c., and

1 oz. cloves, at 13c. 4th. Sold Ephraim B. Price 1 bbl. of salt, at $1.25, 1 bbl. water lime, at $2.25, 50 lbs. coarse salt, at 1¾c., and 20 lbs. mackerel, at 8c.; Peter Brant, 10 yds. muslin de laine, at 50c., 15 yds. factory, at 10c., and 5 spools thread, at 5c.; William Walling, 20 lbs. sugar, at 10c., 10 lbs. coffee, at 10c., and 1 lb. tea, at $1.00. 7th. Sold Merrit Thornton 3 yds. gray cloth, at $1.00, 3 yds. factory, at 8c., and buttons, 6c.; Hiram Mann, 8 lbs. sugar, at 9c., and 5 lbs. coffee, at 14c. 9th. Sold John Messenger cloth and trimmings for overcoat, at $9.00, 6 yds. cassimer, at $2.00 ; and he has paid me cash on account, $20.00. 10th. Sold Albert J. Hovey 10 yds. calico, at 12½c., and 1 spool thread, at 5c.; Alpheus Clark, 1 yd. silk, at $1.25, 1 cord and tassel, at $1.00, and 3 skeins silk, 4c. 11th. Sold Milton Seely 1 ps. factory, 30 yds., at 10c. 12th. Sold John Messenger 50 lbs. sugar, at 10c., and 1 ps. factory, 40 yds., at 8c.; and bought of him 1 firkin butter, at $10.00. 14th. Sold Merrit Thornton cloth and trimmings for pants, at $6.00. 15th. Sold William Walling 3 yds. S. G. cloth, at 56c. 16th. Sold Peter Brant 1 lb. tea, at $1.00, and 10 lbs. sugar, at 10c. 17th. Sold William F. Ashley 9 yds. bed-ticking, at 12½c., and 3 spools, at 5c. 18th. Sold Charles R. Hecox 9 yds. factory, at 9c., 9 yds. ticking, at 12½c., and 2 spools, at 5c. 19th. Sold Samuel Weaver 4 yds. light green broadcloth, at $2.50, 3½ yds. worsted goods, at 75c., and buttons, 50c.; and bought of him 20 lbs. butter, at 15c., and 10 doz. eggs, at 10c. Sold Ephraim B. Price, per wife, 9 yds. muslin de laine, at 25c. 21st. Sold Albert J. Hovey, 1 pair kid gloves, at $1.00 ; Myron Holmes, 1 pair kid gloves, at $1.00. 22d. John Messenger has paid me cash on account, $5.00. 23d. Sold Hiram Mann 8 yds. calico, at 12½c., and 1 spool, at 5c. Peter Brant has paid me cash on account, $10.00. Sold John Hancock 1 lb. tea, at $1.00, 5 lbs. coffee, at 12½c., and 10 lbs. sugar, at 10c. 25th. Sold Milton Seely 3 yds. cassimer, at $2.00, 3 yds. factory, at 8c., and buttons, 6c. 26th. Sold Samuel Moore, per Emogene, 1 pair kid gloves, at $1.00, and 1 pair cotton, at 19c.; William Walling, 10 yds. calico, at 14c., 15 yds. factory, at 10c.; and bought of him 10 cords maple wood, at $2.00. 29th. Sold Peter Brant 15 lbs. sugar, at 10c., and 5 lbs. coffee, at 14c. 30th. Sold Samuel Moore cloth and trimmings for coat, at $9.80, 1

pair suspenders, at 50c., and 1 pair gloves, at 31c.; and he has paid me cash on account, $25.00. Sold Myron Holmes 1 pair buckskin gloves, at $1.00, 1 pair black kid do., at $1.00, cloth and trimmings for dress coat, $15.00, 50 lbs. sugar, at 10c., 20 lbs. coffee, at 15c., 5 lbs. tea, at 50c.; and he has paid me cash on account, $25.00. Bought of him 10 super. plows, at $5.00. 31st. Sold Nathan Brittan 1 pair cotton hose, at 25c., 1 pair worsted gloves, at 50c., and 1 doz. skeins worsted, at 13c.

FEBRUARY

1st. Sold William F. Ashley 1 silk pocket handkerchief, at 50c., and 1 cravat, at $1.50. 4th. Sold Ephraim B. Price 14 yds. shirting, at 12c., 2 yds. linen, at 75c., 4 yds. calico, at 6c., and 1 doz. spools thread, 63c. 5th. Sold Samuel Moore 2 rolls white paper, at 31c., and 3 brooms, at 18c. 6th. Sold Milton Seely 1 satin vest pattern, $3.25, 1 yd. cambric, 10c., 1 white do., 13c., and ½ doz. buttons, at 12c.; Samuel Weaver, 13 yds. shirting, at 13c., 2½ yds. Irish linen, at 88c., and 3 spools thread, at 5c. 7th. Sold Alpheus Clark 10 yds. sheeting, at 10c.; William Walling, 12 yds. calico, at 8c., and 5 lbs. batting, at 12½c. 8th. Sold Ephraim B. Price vest and trimmings, at $2.25, 1 yd. linen, 75c.; and bought of him bill of groceries, $15.42. 9th. Sold William F. Ashley 20 yds. calico, at 12½c. 11th. Sold Merrit Thornton 1 doz. tumblers, $1.00, and 8 lbs. refined sugar, at 12½c.; Nathan Brittan, 12 yds. barred mull, at 31c., and 2 pair cotton hose, at 38c. 13th. Sold John Hancock 1 pair rubbers, at $1.00, 1 pair kid gloves, at $1.00, and 1 pair buskins, at $1.50. 14th. Sold Hiram Mann 1 graduated robe, $3.50, 1 yd. drilling, at 13c., and thread, 6c. 15th. Sold Samuel Moore 32 yds. sheeting, at 10c., and 4 yds. Irish linen, at $1.00. 16th. Sold Albert J. Hovey 1 set fine blue ware, at $3.50; Peter Brant, 1 lb. tea, at $1.00, and 5 lbs. rice, at 5c.; John Messenger, 10 yds. muslin de laine, at 25c., and 1 yd. drilling, at 13c. 18th. Sold Myron Holmes, per son, 1 vest pattern and trimmings, at $8.00. 19th. Sold Charles R. Hecox 17 yds. sheeting, at 5c., and 20 yds. calico, at 12½c. 20th. Sold Samuel Moore 1 fur hat, at $4.00; Milton Seely, per wife, super. shawl, at $30.00; John Hancock, 1 gal. lamp oil, $1.50, and 2 gals. molasses, at 37½c. 21st. Sold Samuel Weaver 2 yds. mull edge, at

31c., and 1 pair gloves, at 75c. 22d. Sold Merrit Thornton 3 yds. cassimer, at $2,00, ¼ yd. canvas, at 19c., and 1 pair black silk gloves, at $1.00. 25th. Sold Alpheus Clark 10 lbs. mackerel, at 8c., 20 lbs. sugar, at 10c., and 10 doz. eggs, at 14c. 27th. Sold Hiram Mann 1 ps. sheeting, 30 yds., at 10c., and 20 yds. calico, at 10c. 28th. Sold Samuel Moore 6 yds. alpaca, at 60c., and 1 yd. cambric, at 10c.; Myron Holmes, 9 yds. muslin de laine, at 37½c., 2 spools thread, at 5c., and 5 skeins silk, at 4c.; William F. Ashley, 1 vest and trimmings, $5.00.

MARCH

1st. Sold Albert J. Hovey 4 lbs. cotton batting, at 12½c., and 8 yds. calico, at 12½c. 2d. Sold Milton Seely 3 yds. edging, at 8c.; E. B. Price, 4 lbs. coffee, at 14c., and 1 lb. cinnamon, at 31c. 4th. Sold Merrit Thornton 2½ yds. linen, at $1.00, 9 yds. gingham, at 38c., and 1 doz. spools, 63c. 6th. Sold John Messenger 1 cap, at $1.50 ; Samuel Weaver, 1 pair rubbers, at $1.75. 7th. Sold Alpheus Clark 1 gal. lamp oil, at $1.00, and 3 lbs. nails, at 8c. 8th. Sold John Hancock 3 bbls. salt, at $1.00, 100 lbs. sugar, at 7½c.; and he has paid me cash on account, $10.00. Sold Peter Brant 2 brooms, at 13c., and 3½ yds. flannel, at 75c. 9th. Sold William Walling 6 yds. alpaca, at 50c., and 1 yd. cambric, at 10c.; and bought of him 10 lbs. butter, at 12½c. 11th. Sold Charles R. Hecox 1 pair kid gloves, $1.00, 1 pair rubbers, at $1.50, 1 pair buskins, at $1.25 ; and bought of him 1 firkin butter, 80 lbs., at 12½c. 12th. Sold Hiram Mann 3 bbls. salt, at $1.00 ; Merrit Thornton, 9 yds. calico, at 12½c.; and bought of him 100 ft. hemlock fence boards, at 7½c. Sold Peter Brant 12 lbs. sugar, at 10c. 13th. Sold Milton Seely, per wife, 12 yds. silk, at $1.25 ; and he has paid me cash on account, $20.00. 14th. Sold William F. Ashley 12 yds. calico, $1.00 ; Myron Holmes, per wife, 1 pair kid buskins, at $1.50. 15th. Sold Samuel Moore 1 set blue ware, at $3.00 ; Samuel Weaver, 1 set fine blue tea ware, at $3.50 ; William Walling, 2 bed-cords, at 25c. 16th. Sold Merrit Thornton ½ bbl. mackerel, at $9.00. 18th. Sold Ephraim B. Price 2 yds. satinet, at 75c. 20th. Sold Peter Brant 4 yds. satinet, at $1.12, and 2 yds. cassimere at $1.50 ; John Hancock, 3 linen handkerchiefs, at 44c., and 1 yd. linen, at 75c. Samuel Weaver, per wife, 1 yd.

Italian silk, at $1.50, 1 cord and tassel, at $1.25, and 3 skeins silk, at 4c. 21st. Sold Milton Seely 1 vest pattern, at $1.50, and trimmings, at 38c. 22d. Sold Albert J. Hovey 9 yds. muslin de laine, at 31c., and 2 skeins silk, at 4c. 23d. Sold Ephraim B. Price 8 yds. gingham, at 50c., 1 yd. cambric, at 10c., and 2 spools thread, at 5c. 25th. Sold Charles R. Hecox 10 yds. gingham, at 31c., and 1 spool thread, at 5c.; John Hancock, 3 linen handkerchiefs, at 31c., and 1 yd. linen, at 75c.; Peter Brant, 14 yds. sheeting, at 11c., 30 yds. do., at 9c., 2 yds. Irish linen, at 75c.; and bought of him 15 lbs. butter, at 12½c. 26th. Sold William Walling 150 lbs. sugar, at 10c. 27th. Sold Samuel Weaver 3 yds. black cassimer, at $2.00; Hiram Mann, cloth and trimmings for dress coat, $15.00; William F. Ashley, 2 pair small shoes, at 31c., and he has paid me cash on account, $5.00. 28th. Sold John Messenger 1 set buttons, at 75c., 1 hank thread, at 13c., and 1 pair shoes, at $1.00. 29th. Sold Myron Holmes 1 shawl, at $10.00, 1 pair kid gloves, at $1.00, 2 yds. mull edging, at 40c., 1 bag clasp, at 50c., and 1 yd. silk velvet, at $3.50; Samuel Moore, 9 yds. silk warp alpaca, at 75c., 1 yd. cambric, at 10c., 1 pair kid buskins, at $1.00, 2 linen handkerchiefs, at 50c., 1 yd. silk, at $1.75, 1 cord and tassel, at 75c. 30th. Sold John Messenger 1 gal. lamp oil, at $1.50. Albert J. Hovey has paid me cash on account, $5.00.

FORM FOR MERCHANTS.

THE principal Books of this Form are the Day-book or Blotter, the Journal, the Ledger, and Cash-book.

The DAY-BOOK and the manner of keeping it are the same as described in the second Form, with these exceptions: the manner and place of dating are different, and it is ruled with single money-columns instead of double.

A PETTY ALPHABET or INDEX to the Day-book should also be kept, in which all the names entered in the Day-book during a month should be entered and alphabetically arranged.

This book should be commenced on the evening of the first business day of each month, by writing in it all the names that were entered in the Day-book during the day, together with the pages on which such entries were made; and so every evening during the month, enter in the Alphabet all the new names that appear in the Day-book, with their pages; and if a name appears that has already been entered in the Alphabet, enter the number of the page on which it stands opposite such name. Whenever the name occurs more than once on the same page of the Day-book, it is indicated in the Alphabet by repeating the number of the page. A small cross (+) placed after the figure indicates that there is a credit-entry on that page in the Day-book.

The JOURNAL is a book into which all the items of each person's account are transferred from the Day-book, and so arranged that those for each month are collected together.

At the close of every month the Day-book should be journalized, which is done in the following manner: Transfer the first entry of the month, in the Day-book, to the Journal; then find the name thus transferred in the Alphabet, and if that has been kept as above directed, you will see on what pages of the Day-book this name again occurs ; then turn to these pages in order, and transfer to the Journal all the items entered to this name, placing them under the name already entered there, with the dates, &c., keeping the debits and credits by themselves. After thus transferring them, place two parallel lines (thus //) opposite each entry on the Day-book, to indicate that they have been carried to the Journal. Proceed in the same manner with the next name in the Day-book, and so on until all is journalized.

After journalizing the month's transactions, the books should be compared to see if the accounts are correctly journalized ; and if found correct, write in the Day-book, after the last entry for the month, Examined.

The LEDGER in this Form is a book in which a whole, or a part of a page, is appropriated to every account in the Journal.

This book is ruled like the Ledger of the second Form, but the lines which there separate the space for the day of the month from the month may be omitted.

An ALPHABET or INDEX to the Ledger, like the one described in the second Form, is necessary.

At the close of the first month the Journal should be posted. But before this is done the Ledger (which we will suppose is new) should be paged, and the names of all the persons (including Stock, Cash, and Merchandise) with whom you have opened an account should be written at the top of the space appropriated to such account. These names, with *Dr.* on the left and *Cr.* on the right, should be written in a bold hand, and then should be alphabetically arranged in the Index, with the page of the Ledger on which they are recorded. The Journal should next be page-marked, which is done as follows : open to the first account in it, and then find in the Alphabet what page of the Ledger is appropriated to this account, and place the number of this page on the margin of the Journal, opposite such account. Proceed in the same manner until each account in the Journal is page-marked.

You are now prepared to post the books. Commence with the first account in the Journal; the figure in the margin shows the page of the Ledger appropriated to this account. Enter on the Dr. side of that page the month in the first space; "To Merchandise" in the wide space, the page of the Journal in the next, and the sum total of the debits in the two next spaces. Then if there are any credits to this account in the Journal, their sum total should be entered in the Ledger on the Cr. side in the same manner, except in the wide space write "By Cash," "By Merchandise," or "By Sundries," as the case may be. Then place two parallel oblique lines, one above and the other below the figure in the margin, to indicate that the account has been posted. Proceed in the same manner until each account in the Journal for the month has been posted. At the close of the next and the subsequent months, the Journal should be posted in the same manner as above described.

Every month, immediately after the Journal has been posted, it should be compared with the Ledger, to see if any mistakes have been made in posting In order to facilitate this, it should be done by two persons. One should take the Journal, and commencing with the first account in the month, give its title and the page of the Ledger upon which it is posted, as indicated by the figures in the margin of the Journal; the other should then turn to this page in the Ledger, and see if it is correctly posted, while the first reads from the Journal the entry, amount, page, &c.

In comparing the books, if any account is found to have been overlooked, it of course should be posted immediately.

If an entry has been made on the wrong side of an account in the Ledger, it should not be erased, but the same amount should be entered on the opposite side of this account "To" or "By Error," and then the entry made as it should have been at first.

If an entry has been posted to the wrong account, the same amount should be entered on the opposite side of this account "To" or "By Error," and it should then be posted in its proper place.

When either the Day-book, Journal, or Ledger is written full, its place is supplied by a new one, and the different books are usually designated by the first letters of the alphabet: the first day-book as Day-book A; the second, Day-book B: the first journal as Journal A; the second, Journal B: the first ledger as Ledger A; the second, Ledger B; the third, Ledger C, &c.

After writing the Day-book for the months of January, February, and March, journalizing and posting it to the Ledger, the accounts may be balanced.

Balancing accounts is placing a sufficient sum on the least side of an account to make it equal with the greatest, and is done by adding the Dr. and Cr. columns, subtracting the least from the greatest, and making the account Dr. "To" or Cr. "By Balance" for the difference. The debit and credit sides will now foot alike. Next draw single lines opposite each other under these columns, and, after adding and placing the amount under them, draw double lines under the amount, to signify that the two sides are balanced and closed; then bring down the balance by making the account Dr. "To" or Cr. "By Balance" of old account. But if the Ledger is full, and you wish to transfer the account to a new one, let the balancing entry be "To" or "By Balance to Ledger B;" and in the new Ledger, "To" or "By Balance from Ledger A."

In the following set of books, after writing the Day-book, journalizing and by posting the three months' transactions, the books may be balanced, and the accounts transferred to a new Ledger.

The same plan will be adopted in this as in the two preceding forms. A portion of the accounts will be in the memoranda form with explanations on one page, and the memoranda, as they appear when entered in the book, on the opposite page. Great care must be taken with this form, otherwise but little if any progress can be made in the second portion of the book. Let the teacher require the pupil to be thoroughly acquainted with the questions that follow, and in examining the books of the pupil rigidly enforce the principles that have been given.

QUESTIONS.

What is this form called? What are the principal books used? What are the Day-book and manner of keeping it like? In what does it differ from the Day-books of the preceding forms? What is the Index to the Day-book called? For what is it used? When should the names entered in the Day-book be placed in this Index? Describe the manner of entering these names. If a name has already been entered, what do you do if it occurs again? What do you do if a name occurs twice on one page? What indicates a credit entry? What is the Journal? How are the accounts arranged in it? When should the Day-book be journalized? What is meant by journalizing? Describe the manner of journalizing. What do the parallel lines (‖) placed opposite the Day-book entry signify? What should be done after journalizing the accounts of the month? If found correct, what do you write in the Day-book? Where do you write it? What is the Ledger in this form? Is it like the Ledger in the preceding forms? What line may be omitted? Is an Alphabet necessary to this Ledger? When should the Journal be posted? What should be written first in the Ledger? What style of writing should be used? What should be placed on the left? What on the right? Where should the names be entered next? How do you page-mark the Journal? After these preparations, what is the manner of posting? What marks do you put in the Journal to show that the account has been posted? After the accounts have been entered, what is to be done? Describe the best way of reviewing the entries? If an account has been overlooked, what is done? Should you erase a wrong entry? How can you correct it? If an entry has been made in the wrong account, how can you correct it? How are the new Day-books, &c., designated when a new set is used? What is meant by balancing accounts? Describe the method. If you open a new account in the same book, how will the entry read? If in a new book?

DAY-BOOK, OR BLOTTER.

MERCHANTS' FORM.

Lyons, Monday, Jan. 3d, 1848.

Pierce & Wilson	Cr.		
By Merchandise per Invoice		173	00
Magie, Sanderson & Co	Cr.		
By Merchandise per Invoice		480	00
Benedict & Rockwell	Cr.		
By Merchandise per Invoice		227	00
——Tuesday, Jan. 4th.——			
Joseph M. Demmon	Dr.		
To 230 Yds. Brown Sheeting	.08	18	40
" 48 " Red Flannel	.38	18	24
" 3 Doz Coat's Sp. Thread.	.48	1	44
Moses Austin	Dr.		
To 17 Yds. Sheeting	.05		85
" 20 " Calico	.13	2	60
——Wednesday, Jan. 5th.——			
George C. Dean	Dr.		
To 10 Yds. M. D. Laine	.31	3	10
" 1 " Drilling			13
" 2 Doz. Buttons	.15		30
——Thursday, Jan. 6th.——			
Nathan Brittan James	Dr.		
To 2 Galls. Lamp Oil	1.25	2	50
" 30 lbs. Loaf Sugar	.13	3	90

MEMORANDA.

Lyons, Monday, Jan. 3d, 1848. Bought of Pierce & Willson merchandise amounting by invoice to $173. Also bought of Sanderson & Co. an invoice of merchandise, $480. Also bought of Benedict & Rockwell an invoice of merchandise, $227. 4th. Sold Joseph M. Demmon 230 yds. brown sheeting, at .08, 48 yds. red flannel, at .38, and 3 doz. Coat's spool thread, at .48 per doz. Also sold Moses Austin 17 yds. sheeting, at .05, and 20 yds. calico, at .13. 5th. Sold George C. Dean 10 yds. muslin de laine, at .31, 1 yd. drilling, .13, and 2 doz. buttons, at .15, per doz. 6th. Sold Nathan Brittan, per James, 2 gallons lamp oil, at 1.25, and 30 lbs. loaf sugar, at .13.

This memoranda would be entered as on the opposite page. The method is the same as employed in the two preceding forms, with the exception, first, of the position of the date, it occupying the centre, and not the side of the page, and the day of the week, as the day of the month being expressed; second, the separate amounts of the different items in each account are placed separately in the last two spaces, and not the sum merely, as in preceding forms. The method of entering the memoranda in Day-book being so similar to the preceding forms, further explanation is deemed unnecessary. The pupil will now carefully enter in his Day-book the following memoranda in connection with the foregoing.

MEMORANDA.

Thursday, January 6th. Sold Rev. Ira Ingraham 5 yds. black broadcloth, at $3.50, 1 satin vest pattern, $5.50, trimmings, $3.75, 5 lbs. of coffee, at $.15, and 10 lbs. of sugar, at $.10. Also sold Miss May Emmonds 3 yds. of linen edging, at $.19. 8th. Sold Hugh Jameson merchandise and rendered bill, $8.07. Also sold John Adams 10 yds. drab fringe, at $.68 and 3 pieces ribbon, at $.31. 10th. Paid Horatio N. Taft's order, $2.38. Sold John M. Holley 3 yards black cassimere, $2.25. Sold Levi S. Fulton 20 lbs. sugar, at $.08, 1 lb. tea, $.88, and he took, also, in cash $8.00. Sold Abram L. Beaumont, 25 lbs. sugar, at $.10. 11th. Sold Moses Austin 7 yds. alpaca, at $.50, 10 yds. cambric, at $.10, 3 skeins silk, at $.04 and 4 sheets of wadding, at $.04. 12th. Sold Samuel Moore 9 yds. muslin de laine, at $.44, 1 yd. cambric, at $.10, 2 yds. drilling, at $.12. Also sold Aaron D. Polhamus, 1 cravat, $1.12. Also sold James C. Smith 4 yds. green baize, at $.50. Also sold Levi S. Fulton 1 pair of fine boots, $5.00. Bought of James Rogers 1 pair fine boots, $5.00. 14th. Sold George C. Youngs 3 yds. black cassimere, at $1.75, and trimmings, $.25. 15th. Sold Moses Austin 30 yds. sheeting, at $.10. 17th. Sold James Rogers 2 hanks linen thread, at $.13, and 4 pieces galoon, at $.31. Sold Nathan Brittan (wife) 1 pair kid gloves, $1.00, 1 pair inferior kid, $.63. Sold Miss Mary Emmonds 9 yds. muslin de laine, at $.31, and trimmings, $.25. She paid cash on account, $2.00. Sold John M. Holley (daughter) 20 skeins zephyr worsted at $.01. Sold Thomas Rook 4 yds. sheep's gray cloth, at $.63. 18th. Sold Moses Austin 10 lbs. cotton yarn, at $.19. Sold George C. Dean (wife) 1 yd. mull edging, $.31, and 1 yd. edging, $.04. 19th. Sold James McElwain 9 yds. muslin de laine, at $.28, 1 yd. cambric, $.10. Sold George C. Youngs ½ lb. tea, at $.88, 1 gallon molasses, at $.44, 1 lb. pepper, at $.13, and 1 lb. spice, at $.13. Bought of George C. Youngs 2 bushels dried plums, at $2.50. 20th. Sold Horatio N. Taft 1 set fine blue tea-ware, $3.50. Sold Levi S. Fulton 1 lb. tea, $.88, 5 lbs rice, at $.05, 1 ounce nutmegs, $.13. 21st. Sold Abram L. Beaumont 1 pair rubbers, $1.00. Sold Rev. Ira Ingraham 1 pair kid gloves, $1.00. Sold Moses Austin 10 lbs. of sugar, at $.10, and 5 lbs. rice, at $.05, and bought of him 5 lbs. butter, at $.13. Sold Nathan Brittan 6 yds. merino, at $1.25. 22d. Sold Samuel Moore 1 yd. figured satin, $3.00, 1¼ yd. twist, at $.04, ¾ yd. black cambric, at $.10, 1 yd. white cambric, $.13, 3 skeins silk, at $.04, 1 sheet wadding, at $.04, ½ doz. buttons, at $.18. 24th. Sold John Adams 185 lbs. sugar, at $.10. Sold Hugh Jameson 6 yds. merino, at $1.12, 5 sheets wadding, at $.04, 4 skeins silk, at $.04. Sold James McElwain 1 lb. tobacco, $.25. 25th. Sold Miss Mary Emmonds 3 yds. Irish linen, at $.52, 4 spools thread, at $.04. 26th. Sold Lucius S. Wood 1 cravat, $.88. Sold Horatio N. Taft 3 yds. black cassimere, $2. 27th. Sold James McElwain 9 yds. ticking, at $.18, 6 yds. tow cloth, at $.31, 16 yds. calico, at $.08, 10 yds. gingham, at $.25. 28th. Sold George C. Dean (wife) 10 yds. calico, at $.18, 2 linen hdkfs., at $.44. Sold John Adams 18 yds. muslin de laine, at $.18. Sold Samuel Moore 1 pair rubbers, $.88, 2 papers pins, at $.10. 29th. Sold Edward Messenger 9 yds. ticking, $.18, 6 yds. tow cloth, at $.31, 11 yds. calico, at $.06, 6 yds. calico, at $.05, and 8 lbs. batting, at $.13. Sold Levi S. Fulton 10 yds. curtain calico, at $.13, 13 yds. calico, at $.06, 4 spools thread, at $.05, 11 yds. alpaca, at $.75, and 1 lb. spice, $.13. 31st. Sold Nathan Brittan 3 linen handkerchiefs, at $.44, and 2 yds. Irish linen, at $.75. Sold Aaron D. Polhamus, 32 yds. shirting, at $.12, 4 yds. Irish linen, at $.75, and 1 doz. spools thread, $.63. Sold Joseph M. Demmon 170 lbs. sugar, at $.10. Abram L. Beaumont 7 yds. flannel, at $.44, and 4 yds. flannel, at $.62. Feb. 1st. Sold Daniel Chapman 4 yds. broadcloth, at $6.00, ½ yd. padding, at $.38, ¾ yd. canvas, at $.25, ½ yd. silk serge, at $1.13, 5 skeins silk, at $.04, and 20 buttons, $.64. Sold James McElwain, 1 bar soap, $.13, and 1 cake fancy soap, $.12. Bought of Jonas W. Goodrich 20 lbs. mackerel, at $.08. Sold Levi S. Fulton 20 lbs. mackerel, at $.08, and 8 lbs. coffee, at $.12. 2d. Sold Abram L. Beaumont (wife) 1 shawl, $7.00. 3d.

Sold Moses Austin 1 comforter, \$.31, and bought of him 8 lbs. butter, at \$.14, and 4 bushels potatoes, at \$.38. Sold Hugh Jameson 3½ yds. flannel, at \$.62. 4th. Sold Ephraim B. Price 4½ yds. coating, at \$2.00, ½ yd. padding, at \$.38, ¾ yd. canvas, at \$.25, 1 set buttons, \$.75, and 1 hank thread, \$.12. 5th. Sold Miss Mary Emmonds, 1 spool thread, \$.05, and 1 thimble, \$.38. Sold George C. Dean 1 looking-glass, \$3.00, and 1 set fine blue tea-ware, \$3.50. 7th. Sold John Adams 31 yds. silk warped alpaca, at \$.52. Sold James Rogers 2 lbs. coffee, at \$.13, 10 lbs. sugar, at \$.10, and 2 gallons molasses, at \$.44. Sold James Bashford 6 tumblers, at \$.12, and 20 lbs. refined sugar, at \$.14. 8th. Sold Abram L. Beaumont 31 yds. brown sheeting, at \$.10. Sold Daniel Chapman 1 pair rubbers, \$.88, and 1 pair kid gloves, \$1.00. 9th. Sold Reuben H. Foster 1 set knives and forks, 2.00, and 1 glass dish, \$1.25, and bought of him 10 bushels potatoes, at \$.44, and 8 bushels oats, at \$.32. 10th. Sold George C. Youngs, ¼ lb. cinnamon, at \$.38, 1 lb. ginger, \$.12, and 1 bbl. salt, \$1.18. Sold Thomas Rook 20 yds. calico, at \$.06, 10 lbs. batting, at \$.11, 5 lbs. cotton yarn, \$.19, and 2 spools thread, at \$.05. Sold Samuel Moore (daughter) 2 yds. mull edging, at \$.40. 11th. Sold Aaron D. Polhamus 9 yds. muslin de laine, at \$.28, 1½ yd. cambric, at \$.10, and ¾ yd. jean, at \$.16. Sold Edmund Hopkins (wife) 1 graduated robe, \$3.50, 1 yd. drilling, \$.13, thread, \$.06, and bought of him 1 geography and atlas, \$1.25. 12th. Sold Daniel Watrous, 1 doz. tumblers, \$1.00, and 8 lbs. refined sugar, at \$.14. Sold George C. Dean (Fellers) ½ ream foolscap paper, \$2.25. Bought of Philip G. Almy merchandise per invoice, \$42.00. 14th. Sold Thomas Ninde ¼ yd. silk serge, \$1.00, and ¼ yd. silk serge, at \$1.12. Sold Ephraim B. Price vest and trimmings, \$2.25, and 1 yd linen, \$.75. 15th. Sold James Rogers 31 yds. sheeting, at \$.10, 2 pieces galoon, at \$.31, and 4 spools thread, at \$.05. Sold Thomas Rook 5 lbs. coffee, at \$.14, and 10 lbs. refined, at \$.14. 16. Sold George C. Youngs, 3 yds. flannel, at \$.50, 9 yds. calico, at \$.13, and 4 spools thread, at \$.05. Sold Nathan Brittan 9 yds. silk warped alpaca, at \$.75, and 1 yd. drilling, at \$.12. Bought of Moses Austin 4 lbs. butter, at \$.14. 17th. Sold Thomas

Ninde (wife) 8 yds. calico, at $.15, and 4 yds. calico, at $.10. Sold James McElwain 1 lb. tobacco, $.25. Sold Thomas E. Dorsey (daughter) 1 bag-clasp, $.50, and 2 linen handkerchiefs, at $.44. Sold Reuben H. Foster 30 yds. brown sheeting, at $.08, and 1 doz. spools thread, $.63. Levi S. Fulton, cash for personal expenses, $15.00. 18th. Sold Edward Messenger 1 vest pattern, $1.00, 1 yd. celecia, $.19, and ½ twilled goods, $.16. Sold Thomas Rook 8 lbs. cotton batting, at $.11, 3 yds. calico, at $.10, and 1 yd. cambric, $.10. 19. Sold Abram L. Beaumont 3½ yds. black broadcloth, at $5.00, ½ yd. padding, at $.38, ¾ canvas, at $.25, 1¼ yd. twist, at $.04, ¼ yd. silk serge, at $1.12, 5 skeins silk, at $.04, and 1 set buttons, $.75. Sold Moses Austin 1 lb. tea, $.88, and 8 lbs. sugar, at $.10. 21st. Sold Levi S. Fulton 10 lbs. sugar, at $.10, and 4 lbs. coffee, at $.14. Sold Edmund Hopkins, 10 lbs. sugar, at $.09, and 1 gallon molasses, $.44. Sold Horatio N. Taft 30 yds. sheeting, at $.10. 22d. Sold Thomas E. Dorsey, 3½ yds. broad cloth, at $3.75, 2 yds. sheeting, at $.11, 10 lbs. sugar, at $.10, and 1 lb. tea, $.88. 23d. Sold James Bashford 33½ lbs. refined sugar, at $.14, and bought of him 2 bush. dried plums, at $2.25, and 5 bush. dried apples, at $.75. Bought of Remsen and Polhamus, wire, $.31. Sold Nathan Brittan 14 lbs. batting, at $.11, and 16 yds. calico, at $.06. Sold Hugh Jameson, ½ lb. tea, at $.88, 1 gallon molasses, at $.44, and 1 lb. of ginger, $.12. Sold James McElwain, 4 lbs. raisins, at $.15, 5 lbs. crushed sugar, at $.14, and 1 oz. nutmegs, at $.13. 24th. Sold George C. Dean 10 yds. sheeting, at $.08½, and 20½ yds. sheeting, at $.10. Sold Samuel Moore 17 yds. calico, at $.16, 10 yds. calico, at $.12. Sold John M. Holley 2 galls. lamp oil, at $1.12, and 1 ball wicking, $.13. Sold James Rogers (Croal), merchandise per order, $3.50. 25th. Sold Jonas W. Goodrich 1 lb. tea, $.75, 1 lb. pepper, $.12, 1 lb. ginger, $.12, and 2 lbs. saleratus, at $.06. 26th. Sold Edward Messenger 6 lbs. cotton yarn, at $.19, and 3 spools thread, at $.05. Sold Reuben H. Foster 7 yds. alpaca, at $.50, 10 yds. cambric, at $.10, 3 skeins silk, at $.04, and 4 sheets wadding, at $.04. 28th. Sold George C. Dean 16 yds. calico, at $.06, 8 lbs. batting, at $.11, and bought of him, 100 lbs. white lead, at $.08. Sold Horatio N. Taft 1 bbl. salt, $1.13. Sold John M. Holley (wife) 1 set knives and forks, $2.25, and 8 yds. flannel, at $.56. 29th. Sold Levi S. Fulton 2½ yds. velvet ribbon, at $.15, and 1 pair kid gloves, $.88. Sold Joseph M. Demmon 19 yds. Canton flannel, at $.40, and 33 yds. shirting, at $.10½. March 1st. Sold Thomas Rook, 4 lbs. cotton batting, at $.11, and 7 yds. calico, at $.08. Sold Thomas E. Dorsey (daughter) 3 yds. edging, at $.08. 2d. Sold Edward Messenger 1½ doz. buttons, at $.50, 1 yd. celecia, $.18, ½ yd. twilled goods, at $.18, and ⅝ yd. canvas, at $.25. Sold Moses Austin 4 lbs. coffee, at $.14, and ¼ lb. cinnamon, at $.38. 3d. Sold Daniel Chapman 2½ yds. linen, at $1.00, 9 yds. gingham, at $.38, and 1 doz. spools thread, at $.63. 4th. Sold Lucius S. Wood 1 pair rubbers, $.88. Sold James C. Smith 1 pair kid gloves, $1.00, 3 linen handkerchiefs, at $.42, and 1 linen handkerchief, 63. 6th. Sold Miss Mary Emmonds 1 pair buskins, $1.13. Sold Abram L. Beaumont 1 pair rubbers, $1.00. Sold Nathan Brittan 1 gallon lamp oil, at $1.25, and 3 lbs. nails, at $.06. 7th. Sold Moses Austin ½ lb. tea, at $1.00, 1 bar soap, $.14, and bought of him, 4½ doz. eggs, at $.11. 8th. Sold, James C. Smith 1 pr. kid buskins, $1.25. Sold John M. Holley 1 yd. silk velvet, $3.50, 1 yd. sheeting, $.15, ⅝ yd. cambric, at $.10, 1 doz. buttons, at $.19, and 3 skeins silk, at $.04. 9th. Sold Daniel Watrous 1 lb. tea, $1.00, and 3 doz. eggs, at $.12. Sold Jonas W. Goodrich 3 yds. cassimere, at $.88, 3 yds. sheeting, at $.10, 1¼ doz. buttons, at $.04, and 3 skeins silk, at $.04. Sold Hugh Jameson 1 cap, $.88. 10th. Sold Thomas Rook 3 lbs. coffee, at $.14, and 1 lb. butter, at $.14. Sold Thomas Ninde ½ ream foolscap paper, $2.25, and 1 quart ink, $.50. Sold Rev. Ira Ingraham 4 linen hdkfs., at $.44. 11th. Sold George C. Youngs ¼ lb. tea, at $.75, 1 lb. pepper, $.12, and 1 gallon molasses, $.44. 13th. Sold Reuben H. Foster (Samuel) 2½ yds. cassimere, at $2.00, 3 yds. sheeting, at $.10, and buttons, $.06. Sold James Bashford 3 bbls. salt, at $1.12, and 100 lbs. sugar, at $.08½. Sold Lucius S. Wood, ½ yd. linen, at $.75. 14th. Sold Aaron D. Polhamus (wife) 1 pr. buskins, $1.13, and 5 yds. muslin de laine, at $.31. 15th. Sold Thomas E. Dorsey (wife) 9 yds. calico, at $18, and bought 9 lbs. butter, at $.14. Sold

James McElwain 1 file, $.10, 1 small file, $.09, and 4 gross screws, at $.44. 16th. Sold Horatio N. Taft 10 yds. gingham, at $.31, and 1 yd. cambric, $.10. Sold Justin W. Burnham (daughter) 8½ yds. calico, at $.12, 6 yds. gingham, at $.34, and trimmings, $.19. 17th. Sold Samuel Moore 1 gall. molasses, $.44, 1 gall. lamp oil, $1.13, and 1 bar soap, $.12. Bought of Remsen and Polhamus 2 boxes glass, at $3.00, and work per Boume, $1.50. Sold George C. Dean (wife) 1 pr. kid gloves, $.63, 1 pr. rubbers, $.88. 18th. Sold Daniel Watrous 3½ yds. black broad cloth, at $5.00, ½ yd. padding, at $.38, ¾ yd. canvas, at $.25, ¼ yd. silk serge, at $1.12, 5 skeins silk, at $.04, and he paid me cash, $12.00. 20th. Sold Moses Austin 2 brooms, $.13, and 3½ yds. flannel, at $.62. 21st. Sold Aaron D. Polhamus 6 yds. alpaca, at $.50, and 1 yd. cambric, $.10. 22d. Sold Miss Mary Emmonds 2 linen hdkfs, at $.38. Sold Nathan Brittan 9 yds. calico, at $.12. Sold Levi S. Fulton 4 lbs. butter, at $.13. Sold Daniel Chapman 14 yds. sheeting, at $.13, 30 yds. sheeting, at $.10, and 2 prs. cotton hose, at $.38. 23d. Sold Reuben H. Foster (wife) 12 yds. blue calico, at $.14. Sold Justin W. Burnham 1 pr. gloves, $.44. Sold Thomas E. Dorsey 3 brooms, at $.13, and 1 patent pail, $.31. 24th. Sold Horatio N. Taft 33 yds. sheeting, at $.09. Sold Thomas Rook 12 yds. curtain calico, at $.12, and 4 spools thread, at $.05. Sold James C. Smith 1 yd. satin vesting, $3.00, ¾ yd. black cambric, at $.10, 1 yd. white cambric, $.13, 1¼ yd. twist, at $.04, ¾ yd. wiggan, at $.12, 2 sheets wadding, at $.04, 4 skeins silk, at $.04, ½ doz. buttons, at $.18. 25th. Sold Aaron D. Polhamus (wife) 12 yds. Italian silk, at $1.25. Sold Samuel Moore (daughter) 1 pr. buskins, $1.12. 27th. Sold Thomas Ninde 1 set fine blue tea-ware, $3.50. Sold John M. Holley 6 yds. flannel, at $.50. 28th. Sold Nathan Brittan 1 pr. red buskins, $1.25. Sold Justin W. Burnham 9 lbs. sugar, at $.10, 4 lbs. rice, at $.05, and 2 lbs. coffee, at $.15. Sold Daniel Chapman 25 lbs. sugar, at $.08, and 10 lbs. coffee, at $.15. Sold James Rogers 32 yds. brown factory, at $.09. 30th. Sold Abram L. Beaumont 31 yds. brown sheeting, at $.09, and 6 spools thread, at $.05. Sold Joseph M. Demmon 128 lbs. coffee, at $.09½. 31st. Sold Levi S. Fulton 9 yds.

muslin de laine, at $.31, and 4 skeins silk, at $.04. Sold Lucius S. Wood 2 linen hdkfs., at $.44. Sold Horatio N. Taft 2 bed cords, at $.25.

INDEX TO THE DAY-BOOK.

MERCHANTS' FORM.

INDEX TO THE DAY-BOOK.

NAMES.	January.	February.	March.
Adams, John			
Almy, Philip G			
Austin, Moses			
Bashford, James			
Beaumont, Abram L			
Benedict & Rockwell			
Brittan, Nathan			
Burnham, Justin W.			
Chapman, Daniel			
Dean, George C.			
Demmon, Joseph M.			
Dorsey, Thomas E.			
Emmonds, Miss M.			
Foster, Reuben H.			
Fulton, Levi S.			
Goodrich, Jonas W.			
Holley, John M.			
Hopkins, Edmund			
Ingraham, Rev. Ira			
Jameson, Hugh			

INDEX TO THE DAY-BOOK.—(Continued.)

NAMES.	January.	February.	March.
Magie, Sanderson & Co.			
McElwain, James			
Messenger, Edward			
Moore, Samuel			
Ninde, Thomas			
Pierce & Wilson			
Polhamus, Aaron D.			
Price, Ephraim B.			
Remson & Polhamus			
Rogers, James			
Rook, Thomas			
Smith, James C.			
Taft, Horatio N.			
Watrous, Daniel			
Wood, Lucius S.			
Youngs, Geo. C.			

The pupil will find the names and months entered in this Index; the figures are left for him to enter according to directions.

Journalizing.

As Journalizing is a process not yet familiar to the student, the memoranda given on the preceding pages are arranged in journal form on the following pages. The student must not merely copy these entries from the Text-book, as that would be a mere exercise in writing. It is expected that he will apply the principles given in the instructions on journalizing in the first part of this form. After he has made the entries as well as he can in his Journal, he may compare it with the form given in the book and correct the error, if any have been made. A good method is to journalize on a slate or paper, and then after correcting, copy the entries into the book. It is of great importance that the teacher should insist upon the pupil's journalizing by the principles, and on no account should he permit him to merely copy from the text-book.

JOURNAL.

MERCHANTS' FORM.

1 # Lyons, January, 1848.

1		Pierce & Wilson	Cr.				
		By Merchandise per Invoice				173	00
1		Magie, Sanderson & Co.	Cr.				
		By Merchandise per Invoice				480	00
2		Benedict & Rockwell	Cr.				
		By Merchandise per Invoice				227	00
2		Joseph M. Demmon	Dr.				
	4	To 230 Yds. B. Sheeting	.08	18	40		
		" 48 " R. Flannel	.38	18	24		
		" 3 Doz. Sp. Thread	.48	1	44		
	31	" 170 lbs. Sugar	.10	17	00	55	08
		Moses Austin	Dr.				
	4	To 17 Yds. Sheeting	.05		85		
		" 20 " Calico	.13	2	60		
	11	" 7 " Alpaca	.50	3	50		
		" 10 " Cambric	.10	1	00		
		" 3 Sks. Silk	.04		12		
		" 4 Sheets Wadding	.04		16		
	15	" 30 Yds. Sheeting	.10	3	00		
	18	" 10 lbs. Cotton Yarn	.19	1	90		
	21	" 10 " Sugar	.10	1	00		
		" 5 " Rice	.05		25	14	38
3		Contra	Cr.				
		By 5 lbs. Butter	.13				65

Lyons, January, 1848.

3		George C. Dean	Dr.				
	5	To 10 Yds. M. D. Laine	.31	3	10		
		" 1 " Drilling			13		
		" 2 Doz. Buttons	.15		30		
	18	" 1 Yd. Mull Edging			31		
		" 1 " Edging			04		
	28	" 10 " Calico	.18	1	80		
		" 2 Linen Hdkfs.	.44		88	6	56
4		Nathan Brittan	Dr.				
	6	To 2 Galls. Lamp Oil	1.25	2	50		
		" 30 lbs. Loaf Sugar	.13	3	90		
	17	" 1 Pr. Kid Gloves		1	00		
		" 1 " do.			63		
	21	" 6 Yds. Merino	1.25	7	50		
	31	" 3 Linen Hdkfs.	.44	1	32		
		" 2 Yds. Irish Linen	.75	1	50	18	35
4		Rev. Ira Ingraham	Dr.				
	6	To 5 Yds. Broad Cloth	3.50	17	50		
		" 1 Satin Vest Pattern		5	50		
		" Trimmings		3	75		
		" 5 lbs. Coffee	.15		75		
		" 10 " Sugar	.10	1	00		
	21	" 1 Pr. Kid Gloves		1	00	29	50
5		Miss Mary Emmonds	Dr.				
	6	To 3 Yds. Linen Edging	.19		57		
	17	" 9 " M. D. Laine	.31	2	79		
		" Trimmings			25		
	25	" 3 Yds. Irish Linen	.52	1	56		
		" 4 Spools Thread	.04		16	5	33

5		Miss Mary Emmonds	Cr.				
	17	By Cash on Acct.				2	00
5		Hugh Jameson	Dr.				
	8	To Merchandise per Bill rend.		8	07		
	24	" 6 Yds. Merino	1.12	6	72		
		" 5 Sheets Wadding	.04		20		
		" 4 Sks. Silk	.04		16	15	15
6		John Adams	Dr.				
	8	To 10 Yds. Drab Fringe	.68	6	80		
		" 3 Ps. Ribbon	.31		93		
	24	" 185 lbs. Sugar	.10	18	50		
	28	" 18 Yds. M. D. Laine	.18	3	24	29	47
6		Horatio N. Taft	Dr.				
	10	To paid your Order		2	38		
	20	" 1 Set F. Blue Tea Ware		3	50		
	26	" 3 Yds. Bk. Cassimer	2.00	6	00	11	88
7		John M. Holley	Dr.				
	10	To 3 Yds. Bk. Cassimer	2.25	6	75		
	17	" 20 Sks. L. Worsted	.01		20	6	95
		Levi S. Fulton	Dr.				
	10	To 20 lbs. Sugar	.08	1	60		
		" 1 " Tea			88		
		" Cash Personal Expenses		8	00		
	12	" 1 Pr. Fine Boots		5	00		
	20	" 1 lb. Tea			88		
		" 5 " Rice	.05		25		
		" 1 oz. Nutmegs			13		
	29	" 10 Yds. Curt. Calico	.13	1	30		

Lyons, January, 1848.

7		Levi S. Fulton	Dr.				
	29	To Amt. brought up		18	04		
		" 13 Yds. Calico	.06		78		
		" 4 Spools Thread	.05		20		
		" 11 Yds. Alpaca	.75	8	25		
		" 1 lb. Spice			13	27	40
8		Abram L. Beaumont	Dr.				
	10	To 25 lbs. Sugar	.10	2	50		
	21	" 1 Pr. Rubbers		1	00		
	31	" 7 Yds. Flannel	.44	3	08		
		" 4 " do.	.62	2	48	9	06
8		Samuel Moore	Dr.				
	12	To 9 Yds. M. D. Laine	.44	3	96		
		" 1 " Cambric			10		
		" 2 " Drilling	.12		24		
	22	" 1 " Figured Satin		3	00		
		" 1¼ " Twist	.04		05		
		" ¾ " Blk. Cambric	.10		08		
		" 1 " White do.			13		
		" 3 Sks. Silk	.04		12		
		" 1 Sheet Wadding			04		
		" ½ Doz. Buttons	.18		09		
	28	" 1 Pr. Rubbers			88		
		" 2 Papers Pins	10		20	8	89
9		Aaron D. Polhamus	Dr.				
	12	To 1 Cravat		1	12		
	31	" 32 Yds. Shirting	.12	3	84		
		" 4 " I. Linen	.75	3	00		
		" 1 Doz. Sp. Thread			63	8	59

Lyons, January, 1848.

9		James C. Smith	Dr.				
	12	To 4 Yds. Green Baize	.50			2	00
10		James Rogers	Cr				
		By 1 Pr. Fine Boots				5	00
		Contra	Dr				
	15	To 2 Hanks L. Thread	.13		26		
		" 4 Ps. Galoon	.31	1	24	1	50
10		George C. Youngs	Dr.				
	14	To 3 Yds. Bk. Cassimer	1.75	5	25		
		" Trimmings			25		
	19	" ½ lb. Tea	.88		44		
		" 1 Gall. Molasses			44		
		" 1 lb. Pepper			13		
		" 1 " Spice			13	6	64
		Contra	Cr.				
		By 2 Bush. D. Plums	2.50			5	00
11		Thomas Rook	Dr.				
	17	To 4 Yds. S. Gray Cloth	.63			2	52
11		James McElwain	Dr.				
	19	To 9 Yds. M. D. Laine	.28	2	52		
		" 1 " Cambric			10		
	24	" 1 lb. Tobacco			25		
	27	" 9 Yds. Ticking	.18	1	62		
		" 6 " Tow Cloth	.31	1	86		
		" 16 " Calico	.08	1	28		
		" 10 " Gingham	.25	2	50	10	13
12		Lucius S. Wood	Dr.				
	26	To 1 Cravat					88

12		Edward Messenger	Dr.		
	29	To 9 Yds. Ticking	.18	1 62	
		" 6 " Tow Cloth	.31	1 86	
		" 11 " Calico	.06	66	
		" 6 " do.	.05	30	
		" 8 lbs. Batting	.13	1 04	5 48

13		Daniel Chapman	Dr.				
	1	To 4 Yds. Broad Cloth	6.00	24	00		
		" ½ " Padding	.38		19		
		" ¾ " Canvas	.25		19		
		" ½ " Silk Serge	1.13		56		
		" 5 Sks. Silk	.04		20		
		" 20 Buttons			64		
	8	" 1 Pr. Rubbers			88		
		" 1 " Kid Gloves		1	00	27	66
11		James McElwain	Dr.				
		To 1 Bar Soap			13		
		" 1 Cake Fancy Soap			12		
	17	" 1 lb. Tobacco			25		
	23	" 4 " Raisins	.15		60		
		" 5 " Crushed Sugar	.14		70		
		" 1 oz. Nutmegs			13	1	93
13		Jonas W. Goodrich	Cr.				
	1	By 20 lbs. Mackerel	.08			1	60
		Contra	Dr.				
	25	To 1 lb. Tea			75		
		" 1 " Pepper			12		
		" 1 " Ginger			12		
		" 2 " Saleratus	.06		12	1	11
		Levi S Fulton	Dr.				
	1	To 20 lbs. Mackerel	.08	1	60		
		" 8 " Coffee	.12		96		
	17	" Cash for Pers. Expenses		15	00		
	21	" 10 lbs. Sugar	.10	1	00		
		" 4 " Coffee	.14		56		
	29	" 2½ Yds. V. Ribbon	.15		38		

7		Levi S. Fulton	Dr.				
	29	To Amt. brought up		19	50		
		" 1 Pr. Kid Gloves			88	20	38
8		Abram L. Beaumont	Dr.				
	2	To 1 Shawl		7	00		
	8	" 31 Yds. Br. Sheeting	.10	3	10		
	19	" 3½ " Broad Cloth	5.00	17	50		
		" ½ " Padding	.38		19		
		" ¾ " Canvas	.25		19		
		" 1¼ " Twist	.04		05		
		" ¼ " Silk Serge	1.12		28		
		" 5 Sks. Silk	.04		20		
		" 1 Set Buttons			75	29	26
3		Moses Austin	Dr.				
	3	To 1 Comforter			31		
	19	" 1 lb. Tea			88		
		" 8 " Sugar	.10		80	1	99
		Contra	Cr.				
	3	By 8 lbs. Butter	.14	1	12		
		" 4 Bush. Potatoes	.38	1	52		
	16	" 4 lbs. Butter	.14		56	3	20
5		Hugh Jameson	Dr.				
	3	To 3½ Yds. Flannel	.62	2	17		
	23	" ½ lb. Tea	.88		44		
		" 1 Gall. Molasses			44		
		" 1 lb. Ginger			12	3	17
		Ephraim B. Price	Dr.				
	4	To 4½ Yds. Coating	2.00	9	00		
		" ½ " Padding	.38		19		

Lyons, February, 1848.

Folio	Day	Particulars	Rate	$	¢	$	¢
14		Ephraim B. Price	Dr.				
	4	To Amt. brought up		9	19		
		" $\frac{3}{4}$ Yd. Canvas	.25		19		
		" 1 Set Buttons			75		
		" 1 Hank Thread			12		
	14	" 1 Vest & Trimmings		2	25		
		" 1 Yd. Linen			75	13	25
5		Miss Mary Emmonds	Dr.				
	5	To 1 Spool Thread			05		
		" 1 Thimble			38		43
3		George C. Dean	Dr.				
		To 1 Looking Glass		3	00		
		" 1 Set F. B. Tea Ware		3	50		
	12	" $\frac{1}{2}$ Ream F. Paper	2.25	1	13		
	24	" 10 Yds. Sheeting	.08$\frac{1}{2}$		85		
		" 20$\frac{1}{2}$ " do.	.10	2	05		
	28	" 16 " Calico	.06		96		
		" 8 lbs. Batting	.11		88	12	37
		Contra	Cr.				
		By 100 lbs White Lead	.08			8	00
3		John Adams	Dr.				
	7	To 31 Yds. S. W. Alpaca	.52			16	12
10		James Rodgers	Dr.				
		To 2 lbs. Coffee	.13		26		
		" 10 " Sugar	.10	1	00		
		" 2 Galls. Molasses	.44		88		
	15	" 31 Yds. Sheeting	.10	3	10		
		" 2 Ps. Galoon	.31		62		
		" 4 Spools Thread	.05		20		

Folio	Date	Account	Rate	$	cts	$	cts
10		James Rogers	Dr.				
	15	To Amt. brought up		6	06		
	24	" Mdse. per Order		3	50	9	56
14		James Bashford	Dr.				
	7	To 6 Tumblers	.12		72		
		" 20 lbs. Ref. Sugar	.14	2	80		
	23	" 33½ " do.	.14	4	69	8	21
		Contra	Cr.				
		By 2 Bush. D. Plums	2.25	4	50		
		" 5 " D. Apples	.75	3	75	8	25
15		Reuben H. Foster	Dr.				
	9	To 1 Set Knives & Forks		2	00		
		" 1 Glass Dish		1	25		
	17	" 30 Yds. Br Sheeting	08	2	40		
		" 1 Doz. Spools Thread			63		
	26	" 7 Yds. Alpaca	.50	3	50		
		" 10 " Cambric	.10	1	00		
		" 3 Sks. Silk	.04		12		
		" 4 Sheets Wadding	.04		16	11	06
		Contra	Cr.				
	9	By 10 Bush. Potatoes	.44	4	40		
		" 8 " Oats	.32	2	56	6	96
10		George C. Youngs	Dr.				
	10	To ¼ lb. Cinnamon	.38		09		
		" 1 " Ginger			12		
		" 1 Bbl. Salt		1	18		
	16	" 3 Yds. Flannel	.50	1	50		
		" 9 " Calico	.13	1	17		
		" 4 Spools Thread	.05		20	4	26

Lyons, February, 1848.

Date	Fol.	Account	Price	$	cts.	$	cts.
11		Thomas Rook	Dr.				
	10	To 20 Yds. Calico	.06	1	20		
		" 10 lbs. Batting	.11	1	10		
		" 5 " Cotton Yarn	.19		95		
		" 2 Sp. Thread	.05		10		
	15	" 5 lbs. Coffee	.14		70		
		" 10 " Ref. Sugar	.14	1	40		
	18	" 8 " Cotton Batting	.11		88		
		" 3 Yds. Calico	.10		30		
		" 1 " Cambric			10	6	73
8		Samuel Moore	Dr.				
	10	To 2 Yds. Mull Edging	.40		80		
	24	" 17 " Calico	.16	2	72		
		" 10 " do.	.12	1	20	4	72
9		Aaron D. Polhamus	Dr.				
	11	To 9 Yds. M. D. Laine	.28	2	52		
		" $1\frac{1}{2}$ " Cambric	.10		15		
		" $\frac{3}{4}$ " Jean	.16		12	2	79
15		Edmund Hopkins	Dr.				
	11	To 1 Graduated Robe		3	50		
		" 1 Yd. Drilling			13		
		" Thread			06		
	21	" 10 lbs. Sugar	.09		90		
		" 1 Gall. Molasses			44	5	03
		Contra	Cr.				
	11	By 1 Geography & Atlas				1	25
16		Daniel Watrous	Dr.				
	12	To 1 Doz. Tumblers		1	00		
		" 8 lbs. Ref. Sugar	.14	1	12	2	12

Lyons, February, 1848.

16		Philip G. Almy	Cr.				
	12	By Mdse. per Invoice				42	00
17		Thomas Ninde	Dr.				
	14	To ¼ Yd. Silk Serge	1.00		25		
		" ¼ " do. do.	1.12		28		
	17	" 8 " Calico	.15	1	20		
		" 4 " do.	.10		40	2	13
4		Nathan Brittan	Dr.				
	16	To 9 Yds. S. W. Alpaca	.75	6	75		
		" 1 " Drilling			12		
	23	" 14 lbs. Batting	.11	1	54		
		" 16 Yds. Calico	.06		96	9	37
17		Thomas E. Dorsey	Dr.				
	17	To 1 Bag Clasp			50		
		" 2 Linen Hdkfs.	.44		88		
	22	" 3½ Yds. Broad Cloth	3.75	13	13		
		" 2 " Sheeting	.11		22		
		" 10 lbs. Sugar	.10	1	00		
		" 1 " Tea			88	16	61
12		Edward Messenger	Dr.				
	18	To 1 Vest Pattern		1	00		
		" 1 Yd. Cilicia			19		
		" ½ " Twilled Goods	.16		08		
	26	" 6 lbs. Cotton Yarn	.19	1	14		
		" 3 Spools Thread	.05		15	2	56
6		Horatio N. Taft	Dr.				
	21	To 30 Yds. Sheeting	.10	3	00		
	28	" 1 Bbl. Salt		1	13	4	13

Lyons, February, 1848.

				$	cts.	$	cts.
18		Remsen & Polhamus Cr.					
	23	By Wire					31
7		John M. Holley Dr.					
	24	To 2 Galls. Lamp Oil	1.12	2	24		
		" 1 Ball Wicking			13		
	28	" 1 Set Knives & Forks		2	25		
		" 8 Yds. Flannel	.56	4	48	9	10
2		Joseph M. Demmon Dr.					
	29	To 19 Yds. Cant. Flannel	.40	7	60		
		" 33 " Shirting	.10½	3	47	11	07

11		Thomas Rook	Dr.				
	1	To 4 lbs. Cotton Batting	.11		44		
		" 7 Yds. Calico	.08		56		
	10	" 3 lbs. Coffee	.14		42		
		" 1 " Butter			14		
	24	" 12 Yds. Curt. Calico	.12	1	44		
		" 4 Spools Thread	.05		20	3	20
17		Thomas E. Dorsey	Dr.				
	1	To 3 Yds. Edging	.08		24		
	15	" 9 " Calico	.18	1	62		
	23	" 3 Brooms	.13		39		
		" 1 Patent Pail			31	2	56
		Contra	Cr.				
	15	By 9 lbs. Butter	.14			1	26
12		Edward Messenger	Dr.				
	2	To 1¼ Doz. Buttons	.50		62		
		" 1 Yd. Celecia			18		
		" ½ " Twilled Goods	.18		09		
		" ¾ " Canvas	.25		19	1	08
3		Moses Austin	Dr.				
	2	To 4 lbs. Coffee	.14		56		
		" ¼ " Cinnamon	.38		09		
	7	" ½ " Tea	1.00		50		
		" 1 Bar Soap			14		
	20	" 2 Brooms	.13		26		
		" 3½ Yds. Flannel	.62	2	17	3	72
		Contra	Cr.				
	7	By 4¼ Doz. Eggs	.11				47

15 Lyons, March, 1848.

Folio	Date	Particulars	Price	$	cts.	$	cts.
13		Daniel Chapman Dr.					
	3	To 2½ Yds. Linen	1.00	2	50		
		" 9 " Gingham	.38	3	42		
		" 1 Doz. Spools Thread			63		
	22	" 14 Yds. Sheeting	.13	1	82		
		" 30 " do.	.10	3	00		
		" 2 Pr. Cotton Hose	.38		76		
	29	" 25 lbs. Sugar	.08	2	00		
		" 10 " Coffee	.15	1	50	15	63
12		Lucius S. Wood Dr.					
	4	To 1 Pr. Rubbers			88		
	13	" ½ Yd. Linen	.75		38		
	31	" 2 Linen Hdkfs.	.44		88	2	14
9		James C. Smith Dr.					
	4	To 1 Pr. Kid Gloves		1	00		
		" 3 Linen Hdkfs.	42	1	26		
		" 1 do. do.			63		
	8	" 1 Pr. Kid Buskins		1	25		
	24	" 1 Yd. Satin Vesting		3	00		
		" ¾ " Blk. Cambric	.10		08		
		" 1 " White do.			13		
		" 1¼ " Twist	.04		05		
		" ¾ " Wiggan	.12		09		
		" 2 Sheets Wadding	.04		08		
		" 4 Sks. Silk	.04		16		
		" ½ Doz. Buttons	.18		09	7	82
5		Miss Mary Emmonds Dr.					
	6	To 1 Pr. Buskins		1	13		
	22	" 2 Linen Hdkfs.	.38		76	1	89

Lyons, March, 1848.

Fol.	Day	Particulars	Price	$	cts.	$	cts.
8		Abram L. Beaumont Dr.					
	6	To 1 Pr. Rubbers		1	00		
	30	" 31 Yds. Br. Sheeting	.09	2	79		
		" 6 Spools Thread	.05		30	4	09
4		Nathan Brittan Dr.					
	6	To 1 Gall. Lamp Oil		1	25		
		" 3 lbs. Nails	.06		18		
	22	" 9 Yds. Calico	.12	1	08		
	28	" 1 Pr. Kid Buskins		1	25	3	76
7		John M. Holley Dr.					
	8	To 1 Yd. Silk Velvet		3	50		
		" 1 " Sheeting			15		
		" $\frac{3}{4}$ " Cambric	.10		08		
		" 1 Doz. Buttons			19		
		" 3 Sks. Silk	.04		12		
	27	" 6 Yds. Flannel	.50	3	00	7	04
16		Daniel Watrous Dr.					
	9	To 1 lb. Tea		1	00		
		" 3 Doz. Eggs	.12		36		
	18	" $3\frac{1}{2}$ Yds. B. B. Cloth	5.00	17	50		
		" $\frac{1}{2}$ " Padding	.38		19		
		" $\frac{3}{4}$ " Canvas	.25		19		
		" $\frac{1}{4}$ " Silk Serge	1.12		28		
		" 5 Sks. Silk	.04		20	19	72
		Contra Cr.					
		By Cash				12	00
		Jonas W. Goodrich Dr.					
	9	To 3 Yds. Cassimer	.88	2	64		
		" 3 " Sheeting	.10		30		

17 Lyons, March, 1848.

13		Jonas W. Goodrich	Dr.				
	9	To Amt. brought up		2	94		
		" 1¼ Doz. Buttons	.04		05		
		" 3 Sks. Silk	.04		12	3	11
5		Hugh Jameson	Dr.				
	9	To 1 Cap					88
17		Thomas Ninde	Dr.				
	10	To ½ Ream F. Paper	2.25	1	13		
		" 1 Quart Ink			50		
	27	" 1 Set F. Blue Tea Ware		3	50	5	13
4		Rev. Ira Ingraham	Dr.				
	10	To 4 Linen Hdkfs	.44			1	76
10		George C. Youngs	Dr.				
	11	To ½ lb. Tea	.75		38		
		" 1 " Pepper			12		
		" 1 Gall. Molasses			44		94
15		Reuben H. Foster	Dr.				
	13	To 2½ Yds. Cassimer	2.00	5	00		
		" 3 " Sheeting	.10		30		
		" Buttons			06		
	23	" 12 Yds. Blue Calico	.14	1	68	7	04
14		James Bashford	Dr.				
	13	To 3 Bbls. Salt	1.12	3	36		
		" 100 lbs. Sugar	.08½	8	50	11	86
		Aaron D. Pelhamus	Dr.				
	14	To 1 Pr. Buskins		1	13		

Ref.	Day	Account / Item	Rate	$	cts.	$	cts.
9		Aaron D. Polhamus Dr.					
	14	To Amt. brought up		1	13		
		" 5 Yds. M. D. Lainè	.31	1	55		
	21	" 6 " Alpaca	.50	3	00		
		" 1 " Cambric			10		
	25	" 12 " Italian Silk	1.25	15	00	20	78
11		James McElwain Dr.					
	15	To 1 File			10		
		" 1 do.			09		
		" 4 Gross Screws	.44	1	76	1	95
6		Horatio N. Taft Dr.					
	16	To 10 Yds. Gingham	.31	3	10		
		" 1 " Cambric			10		
	24	" 33 " Sheeting	.09	2	97		
	31	" 2 Bed Cords	.25		50	6	67
18		Justin W. Burnham Dr.					
	16	To 8½ Yds. Calico	.12	1	02		
		" 6 " Gingham	.34	2	04		
		" Trimmings			19		
	23	" 1 Pr. Gloves			44		
	28	" 9 lbs. Sugar	.10		90		
		" 4 " Rice	.05		20		
		" 2 " Coffee	.15		30	5	09
8		Samuel Moore Dr.					
	17	To 1 Gall. Molasses			44		
		" 1 " Lamp Oil		1	13		
		" 1 Bar Soap			12		
	25	" 1 Pr. Buskins		1	12	2	81

Lyons, March, 1848.

18		Remsen & Polhamus	Cr.				
	17	By 2 Boxes Glass	3.00	6	00		
		" Work per Bourne		1	50	7	50
3		George C. Dean	Dr.				
	17	To 1 Pr. Kid Gloves			63		
		" 1 " Rubbers			88	1	51
7		Levi S. Fulton	Dr.				
	22	To 4 lbs. Butter	.13		52		
	31	" 9 Yds. M. D. Laine	.31	2	79		
		" 4 Sks. Silk	.04		16	3	47
10		James Rogers	Dr.				
	29	To 32 Yds. Bro. Factory	.09			2	88
2		Joseph M. Demmon	Dr.				
	30	To 128 lbs. Coffee	.09½			12	16

INDEX TO THE LEDGER.

MERCHANTS' FORM.

A

Adams, John
Almy, Philip G.
Austin, Moses

B

Bashford, James
Beaumont, Abram L.
Benedict & Rockwell
Brittan, Nathan
Burnham, Justin W.

C

Chapman Daniel

D

Dean, George C.
Demmon, Joseph M.
Dorsey, Thomas E.

E

Emmonds, Miss M.

F

Foster, Reuben H.
Fulton, Levi S.

G

Goodrich, Jonas W.

H

Holley, John M.
Hopkins, Edmund

I

Ingraham, Rev. Ira

T	X
Taft, Horatio N.	
V	**Y**
	Youngs, Geo. C.
W	**Z**
Watrous, Daniel *Wood, Lucius S.*	

LEDGER.

MERCHANTS FORM.

Dr.		Pierce & Wilson							Cr. 1
1848 Mar.	To Balance Ledger B. page	1	173	00	1848 Jan.	By Merchandise	1	173	00

Dr.		Magie, Sanderson & Co.							Cr.
1848 Mar.	To Balance Ledger B. page	1	480	00	1848 Jan.	By Merchandise	1	480	00

2 Dr. **Benedict & Rockwell** Cr.

Date		Fol.	$	cts.	Date		Fol.	$	cts.
1848 Mar.	To Balance Ledger B. page	2	227	00	1848 Jan.	By Merchandise	1	227	00

Dr. **Joseph M Demmon** Cr.

Date		Fol.	$	cts.	Date		Fol.	$	cts.
1848 Jan.	To Merchandise	1	55	08	1848 Mar	By Balance Ledger B. page	2	78	31
Feb.	" do.	13	11	07					
Mar.	" do.	19	12	16					
			78	31				78	31

Dr. **Moses Austin** Cr. 3

1848					1848				
Jan	To Merchandise	1	14	38	Jan.	By Butter	1		65
Feb.	" do.	8	1	99	Feb.	" Sundries	8	3	20
Mar.	" do	14	3	72	Mar.	" Eggs	14		47
					"	" Balance Ledger B.	3	15	77
			20	09				20	09

Dr. **George C. Dean** Cr.

1848					1848				
Jan.	To Merchandise	2	6	56	Feb.	By Merchandise	9	8	00
Feb.	" do.	9	12	37	Mar.	" Balance Ledger B.	3	12	44
Mar.	" do.	19	1	51					
			20	44				20	44

The pupil will perceive at once that the principles of posting are the same as in the two preceding forms. The accounts are posted from the Journal, and as in accounts on opposite page: first, the name is written, with Dr. on the left hand, and Cr. on the right; second, the date, year and month is placed in first space; the article in the second space, the page of the Journal in the third space, and the sum, or amount of the month's dealings, as per Journal, in the fourth and fifth spaces. The students will notice that the account of Pierce & Wilson is balanced, "Mar. To Bal. Ledger B, page 1, $173." This entry is made on the supposition, that the accounts are to be transferred from this Ledger to another; this Ledger, as the first, is Ledger A, and the second would be called Ledger B. The accounts of Pierce & Wilson; Magie, Sanderson & Co.; Benedict & Rockwell, Joseph M. Demon, Moses Austin, and George C. Dean are given to guide the pupil. The others if properly posted, will require the following amounts to balance them: Nathan Brittan, $31.48; Rev. Ira Ingraham, $31.26; Miss Mary Emmonds, $5.65; Hugh Jameson, $19.20; John Adams, $45.59; Horatio N. Taft, $22.68; John M. Holley, $23.09; Levi S. Fulton, $51.25; Abram L. Beaumont, $42.41; Samuel Moore, $16.42; Aaron D. Polhamus, $32.16; James C. Smith, $9.82; James Rogers, $8.94; George C. Youngs, $6.84; Thomas Rook,, $12.45; James McElwain, 14.01; Lucius S. Wood, $3.02; Edward Messenger, $9.12; Daniel Chapman, $43.29; Jonas W. Goodrich, $2.62; Ephraim B. Price, $13.25; James Bashford, $11.82; Reuben H. Foster, $11.14; Edmund Hopkins, $3.78; Daniel Watrous, $9.84; Philip G. Almy, $42.00; Thomas Ninde, $7.26; Thomas E. Dorsey, $17.91; Remsen & Polhamus, $7.81; Justin W. Burnham, $5,09.

The pupil will balance these accounts, by making the entries as in the examples given "To or By balance, Ledger B," as the amount is to be credited, or debited, in New Ledger.

PRACTICAL EXERCISES.

MERCHANTS' FORM.

For the purpose of giving a more practical knowledge of the foregoing form of books, we have given on the following pages a Memorandum of the transactions as they occurred, for the months of April, May, and June, giving the price per yard, pound, ounce, gallon, or piece, leaving the amount to be extended by the learner.

Before commencing the Day-Book, transfer the balances from the last Ledger to the new one, making the persons that are indebted to you debtor "To Balance from Ledger A," and the persons to whom you are indebted credit "By Balance from Ledger A," placing the number of the page from whence the account was transferred in the column appropriated for that purpose, so that, in case of necessity, the old account may be more readily referred to.

The transactions on the following pages may now be recorded in the blank Day-Book in the same manner as in the preceding form. After writing one month, Journalize and Post it, according to the directions previously given.

If the balances of the accounts in Ledger A are properly transferred to Ledger B, and the transactions on the following pages correctly recorded, journalized, and posted, the accounts in Ledger B will, with the exception of the account of Levi S. Fulton, all balance.

The learner may, if he chooses, substitute his own name for that of Levi S. Fulton; and instead of Lyons, at the top of the page in the Day-Book and Journal, he may insert his own place of residence.

MEMORANDUM.

APRIL

1st. Bot. of Remsen & Polhamus 4 lbs. wrought nails, at 16c. Sold Horatio N. Taft, per wife, 10 yds. gingham, at 31c. 3d. Sold Ephraim B. Price 2 yds. satinet, at 75c.; Rev. Ira Ingraham, per daughter, 3 linen handkerchiefs, at 44c., and 1 yd. linen, at 75c. 4th. Sold George C. Dean, per wife, 8 yds. gingham, at 31c., 1 yd. cambric, at 10c., and 2 spools thread, at 5c. 5th. Sold Moses Austin 1 oz. nutmegs, at 13c., and 3 yds. sheeting, at 10c.; James McElwain, 4 yds. satinet, at $1.12, and 2 yds. cassimer, at $1.50. 6th. Sold Daniel Watrous 4 lbs. butter, at 14c.; Abram L. Beaumont, 2 pair small shoes. at 56c.; Thomas E. Dorsey, 14 yds. sheeting, at 11c., 30 yds. sheeting, at 9c., and 2 yds. Irish linen, at 75c. Bot. of Thomas E. Dorsey 14 lbs. butter, at 14c. 7th. Sold John Adams 150 lbs. sugar, at 9c. 8th. Sold Samuel Moore 9 yds. flannel, at 50c.; Miss Mary Emmonds, 3 yds. velvet ribbon, at 13c., and 1 pair silk gloves, at 63c., and she has paid me $6.67 to balance her account. 10th. Sold Thomas Rook 1 set buttons, at 75c., 1 hank thread, at 13c., 1 pair buskins, at $1.13, 9 yds. calico, at 12c., and 3 skeins silk, at 4c. 11th. Sold Horatio N. Taft 1 looking-glass, at $8.00; Thomas E Dorsey, 2 yds. calico, at 8c., 7 lbs. coffee, at 10c., 2 lbs. refined sugar, at 14c., and 1 lb. Young Hyson tea, at 88c. 12th. Sold Ephraim B. Price 9 yds. calico, at 19c., and 3 yds. calico, at 10c.; Jonas W. Goodrich, 3 yds. black cassimer, at $2.00; John M. Holley, per wife, 10 yds. calico, at 15c., 2 linen handkerchiefs, at 40c., and 8 window glass, at 5c. 13th. Bot. of Remsen & Polhamus a bill of goods amounting to $13.10. Sold James McElwain, per Newson, 12 yds. calico, at 12c. 14th. Sold Nathan Brittan 1 gallon lamp oil, at $1.25. Bought of Moses Austin 10 lbs. butter, at 14c., 4 doz. eggs, at 10c. Sold Levi S. Fulton 6 lbs. butter, at 14c.; Rev. Ira Ingraham, per wife, 4 yds. ribbon, at 20c., and 4 skeins silk, at 4c. 15th. Sold Justin W. Burnham 3 yds. cambric, at 10c., and 2 yds. green baize, at 50c.; John Adams, 26 yds. muslin de laine, at 25c. 17th. Sold George C. Dean 6 yds. cambric, at 10c., and 3 yds. drilling, at 12c. 18th. Sold Daniel Watrous 2 sheets pasteboard, at 10c., and 5 yds. ribbon, at 15c.; Abram L. Beaumont, per wife, 3 yds. bonnet ribbon, at 55c., and 4 skeins silk, at 4c. 19th. Sold James Rogers 5 lbs. butter, at 14c. Bot. of James Rogers 1 pair gaiter boots, at $2.00. Sold Horatio N. Taft 1 pair kid gloves, at $1.00, and 2 linen handkerchiefs, at 44c. Bot. of John Adams a bill of goods for L. S. Wood, $3.75. 20th. Sold John M. Holley $\frac{1}{4}$ lb.

cinnamon, at 38c., 5 lbs. raisins, at 18c., and 1 oz. nutmegs, at 12c. Sold Rev. Ira Ingraham 7 yds. carpeting, at 85c. 21st. Sold George C. Dean 2¾ yds. cassimer, at $1.50, and 1 yd. sheeting, at 10c. Sold Jonas W. Goodrich 12 yds. calico, at 20c., and 1 hank thread, at 15c. 22d. Sold James McElwain 12 lbs. sugar, at 9c., 5 lbs. Old Java coffee, at 15c., and 2 lbs. tea, at 75c. Paid Lucius S. Wood, cash, $25.00. 24th. Sold Samuel Moore 1 set knives and forks, at $2.75. Samuel Moore has paid me cash, on account, $12.00. Sold Thomas E. Dorsey 2 gals. molasses, at 50c. Bot. of Thomas E. Dorsey 8 lbs. butter, at 13c.; and he has paid me cash, on account, $5.00. Sold Aaron D. Polhamus 7 lbs. cotton yarn, at 20c., and 11 yds. calico, at 15c. 26th. Sold Daniel Watrous 16 yds. shirting, at 12c., and 1½ yd. Irish linen, at 75c.; Abram L. Beaumont, 11 yds. gingham, at 28c., and 2 yds. drilling, at 11c. 27th. Sold Nathan Brittan 1 patent pail, at 31c., 1 washtub, at $1.25, 6 brooms, at 13c.; and he has paid me cash, on account, $8.00. 28th. Sold James C. Smith 3 yds. black cassimer, at $2.25, 1 yd. sheeting, at 12c., and buttons, at 6c.; Reuben H. Foster, 1 lb. Young Hyson tea, at 88c. 29th. Sold Thomas Rook 27 yds. sheeting, at 10c. Bot. of Thomas Rook 12 lbs. butter, at 13c., and 4 doz. eggs, at 9c. Sold Levi S. Fulton 5 lbs. butter, at 13c., and 2 doz. eggs, at 9c.; Horatio N. Taft, 9 yds. ticking, at 19c., 1 hank thread, at 12c.; and he has paid me cash, on account, $10.00. 29th. Sold Justin W. Burnham 6 yds. merino, at $1.25, 8 yds. cambric, at 10c., 4 sheets wadding, at 4c., and 4 skeins silk, at 4c. Sent Pierce & Wilson, New York, draft at sight on H. Dwight, jr., for $173.00; Magie, Sanderson, & Co., New York, a draft at 10 days' sight, on H. Dwight, jr., for $480.00; Benedict & Rockwell, New York, a draft at sight on H. Dwight, jr., for $227.00.

MAY

1st. Sold Justin W. Burnham 3½ yds. bonnet ribbon, at 44c.; and he has paid me cash, to balance his account, $16.55. 2d. Sold Daniel Watrous 1 gross screws, at 44c.; John M. Holley, 1 pair kid gloves, at $1.00; Thos. Ninde, 3½ yds. calico, at 15c., 2½ yds. do., at 18c., 1 paper pins, at 10c., 10 lbs. sugar, at 10c.; and he has paid me cash, to balance his account, $9.34. 3d. Sold John M. Holley, per wife, 6 yds. alpaca, at 75c., and 1 pair gloves, at 44c.; Daniel Chapman, $2\frac{3}{8}$ yds. linen, at 75c., 3 yds. flannel, at 62c., and one pair gloves, at 44c.; Moses Austin, 30 yds. sheeting, at 10c. 4th. Sold Remsen & Polhamus $3\frac{1}{2}$ yds. satinet, at $1.00; Edward Messenger, $2\frac{1}{2}$ yds. cambric, at 10c., 3 lbs. batting, at 11c., and $1\frac{1}{2}$ doz. buttons, at 25c. 5th. Sold Thomas E. Dorsey 8 yds. sheeting, at 10c., 9 yds. do., at 15c., $1\frac{1}{4}$ yds. silk, at $1.00, 3 yds. ribbon, at 25c., 2 oz. indigo, at 13c., and 1 whitewash brush, at 63c. Edward Messenger has paid me cash, to balance his account, $10.08. 6th. Sold Edmund Hopkins, per wife, 10 yds. calico, at 15c., and 6 yds. do. at 10c. 8th. Sold Reuben H. Foster 17 yds. sheeting, at 11c.; Jonas W. Goodrich, 12 yds. calico, at 8c., and $5\frac{1}{2}$ lbs. batting, at 12c. 9th. Sold Ephraim B. Price 4 yds. cambric, at 10c., and 2 yds. drilling at 13c. Bot. of Ephraim B. Price 8 lbs. codfish, at $4\frac{1}{2}$c. Sold Levi S. Fulton 8 lbs. codfish, at $4\frac{1}{2}$c. Paid him cash, for personal expenses, $14.75. 10th. Sold John M. Holley, per daughter, 1 dress handkerchief, at $1.25, 1 linen handkerchief, at 40c., and 4 yds. cambric, at 10c. 11th. Sold Samuel Moore, per daughter, 1 parasol, at $2.50, and 1 paper pins, at 10c.; Horatio N. Taft, 1 lb. Young Hyson tea, at 88c. 12th. Sold Abram L. Beaumont, per Ellen, 1 yd. ribbon, at 25c., 5 yds. do., at 8c., and 5 yds. edging, at 15c.; John M. Holley, per wife, 4 yds. black silk edging, at 44c.; Edmund Hopkins, 4 yds. shirting, at 12c.; and he has paid me cash, to balance his account, $6.36. 13th. Sold Thomas E. Dorsey, per daughter, 1 China hat, at $3.75; and bought of him 8 lbs. butter, at 13c. 16th. Sold James McElwain 14 lbs. butter, at 13c., and 2 lbs. Young Hyson tea, at 88c. 17th. Sold Reuben H. Foster, per Susan, 1 parasol, at $2.00; Moses Austin, per wife, 4 lbs. batting, at 11c., $1\frac{1}{2}$ doz. buttons, at 25c., 3 yds. ribbon, at 15c.; and bought of him 16 lbs. butter, at 13c. 18th. Sold Jonas W. Goodrich, per Melville, 1 vest pattern, at 88c., and trimmings, at 38c. 19th. Sold Samuel Moore 10 lbs. nails, at 6c.; James Rogers, per wife, 4 yds. toweling, at 10c., 9 yds. shirting, at 15c., 3 yds. drilling, at 12c., 3 spools thread, at 5c., and 3 skeins silk, at 4c. 20th. Sold Abram L. Beaumont 1 roll window paper, at 31c., 1 roll tape, at 6c., 6 yds. French calico, at 25c., and 2 yds. ribbon, at 5c.; John Adams, per son, 26 yds. gingham, at 30c.; George C. Dean, 10 lbs. cotton yarn, at 20c. 22d. Sold Nathan Brittan 1 paper black tea, at 44c.; Levi S. Fulton, 9 yds. ticking, at 15c.; Ephraim B. Price, 10 yds. French calico, at 25c. 23d. Sold James McElwain, per wife, 1 parasol, at $2.25, 2 linen handkerchiefs, at 38c., 2 pair cotton hose, at 20c., and 2 papers pins, at 10c. 24th. Sold James C. Smith 8 lbs. rice, at 5c., 2 lbs. tea, at 88c., 8 lbs. Old Java coffee, at 15c., and 4 lbs. refined sugar, at 14c. 25th. Sold Daniel Watrous 1 pair kid gloves, at $1.00; Lucius S. Wood, 1 pair kid gloves, at 88c.; Levi S. Fulton, 2 linen handkerchiefs, at 44c. 26th. Sold Daniel Chapman 1 cravat, at $1.13, and 3 linen handkerchiefs, at 88c. 27th. Sold Ephraim B. Price 6 yds. merino, at $1.25, and 7 skeins silk, at 4c. 30th. Sold Nathan Brittan 2¾ yds. cassimer, at $2.00; Joseph M. Demmon, 20 lbs. cotton batting, at 9½c. 31st. Sold James Rogers 8 yds. jean, at 16c.; George C. Dean, 6 yds. flannel, at 44c., and 2 yds. Irish linen, at 75c.

JUNE

1st. Sold Abram L. Beaumont 7 yds. blue calico, at 12c., 12½ yds. summer goods, at 23c., 6 yds. factory, at 10c., 10 lbs. cotton yarn, at 20c., 1¼ doz. buttons, at 4c., and 1 hank linen thread, at 13c.; Nathan Brittan, 2 pair cotton hose, at 38c. 2d. Sold Moses Austin 2 rolls window paper, at 31c., and 2 palm leaf hats, at 20c.; and he has given me his note at 30 days, to balance his account, for $17.61. Sold John Adams 4 bbls. salt, at $1.00, 32 lbs. refined sugar, at 13c.; and he has paid me cash, to balance his account, $77.80. 3d. Sold James Rogers 4 yds. gimp, at 25.; John M. Holley, 11 yds. lawn, at 31c., 1 yd. drilling, at 13c., and 2 pair whalebones, at 4c. 5th. Sold Thomas Rook 1 vest pattern, at 75c., 2½ yds. cassimer, at $1.00, 5 yds. lawn, at 20c., 1 pair walking shoes, at $1.00, 1 bonnet, at $3.00, 2 spools thread, at 5c., and 4 lbs. coffee, at 10c. Bot. of him 37¼ lbs. butter, at 13c., 8 doz. eggs, at 10c.; and he has paid me cash, to balance his account, $19.55. 6th. Bot. of George C. Youngs 20 lbs. ham, at 8½c., 31 lbs. do., at 8c.; and he has paid me cash, to balance his account, $2.66. Sold Lucius S. Wood 5 yds. brown linen, at 31c., and thread, at 6c. 7th. Sold James Rogers 10 yds. linen gingham, at 38c., 6 yds. sheeting, at 11c., 2 yds. edging, at 15c., and 2 skeins silk, at 4c.; Ephraim B. Price, per wife, 1 parasol, at $2.25. 8th. Sold James McElwain 1 bar soap, at 16c.;

Daniel Watrous, 4 yds. linen goods, at 31c., buttons, at 6c.; and he has paid me cash, to balance his account, $17.14. 9th. Sold Thomas E. Dorsey, per Juliet, purse twist, 75c., and steel beads, 75c.; George C. Dean, 2¼ yds. gingham, at 31c. 10th. Sold Nathan Brittan 12 yds. barred mull, at 31c., 2 pair cotton hose, at 38c.; and he has given me his note at 3 months, to balance his account, for $38.25. 12th. Sold Abram L. Beaumont 8 lbs. nails, at 6c.; John M. Holley, 3 yds. edging, at 8c., 3 spools thread, at 5c., and 2 skeins silk, at 4c. James Bashford has paid me cash, to balance his acconnt, $11.82. 13th. Sold Daniel Chapman 10 yds. alpaca, at 75c., 10¾ yds. calico, at 7c., 1 yd. cambric, at 10c., and 1 yd. drilling, at 13c. Paid Levi S. Fulton cash, for personal expenses, $25.00. 14th. Sold James C. Smith 13 yds. shirting, at 13c., 2½ yds. Irish linen, at 88c., 5½ yds. calico, at 7c., 3 spools thread, at 5c., and 4 skeins silk, at 4c. George C. Dean has paid me cash, to balance his account, $27.14. 15th. Sold Reuben H. Foster 2 gals. molasses, at 44c. and 1 gal. lamp oil, at $1.00. 16th. James McElwain has given me his note at 3 months, to balance his account, for $33.61. Sold Aaron D. Polhamus 1 yd. satin vesting, at $3.25, 1 yd. black cambric, at 10c., 1 yd. white do., at 13c., and ½ doz. buttons, at 25c. 17th. Sold Thomas E. Dorsey 8 yds. blue calico, at 13c., 4 yds. sheeting, at 8c., 3 lbs. batting, at 12c. Bot. of him 18½ lbs. butter, at 13c.; and he has paid me cash, to balance his account, $27.24. 19th. Reuben H. Foster has given me his note at 3 months, to balance his account, for $17.77. Sold Samuel Moore 2 rolls window paper, at 31c., 3 brooms, at 18c.; and he has given me his note at 30 days, to balance his account, for $16.03. 20th. Sold Ephraim B. Price 14 yards. shirting, at 12c., 2 yds. linen, at 75c., 4 yds. calico, at 6c., and 1 doz. spools thread, at 63c. 21st. Sold Abram L. Beaumont 11 yds. Oregon plaid, at 31c., 1 yd. drilling, at 13c., ½ yd. cambric, at 10c., 1 spool thread, at 5c.; and he has given me his note at 60 days, to balance his account, for $62.63. 22d. Daniel Chapman has paid me cash, to balance his account, $59.62. Sold Jonas W. Goodrich 9 yds. gingham, at 28c., trimmings, at 31c.; and he has paid me cash, to balance his account, $16.88. 23d. John M. Holley has given me his note at 6 months, to balance his account, for $40.74. Sold Rev. Ira Ingraham 4 pair cotton hose, at 40c.; and he has paid me cash, to balance his account, $41.84. 24th. Sold Hugh Jameson 3 yds. satinet, at 75c. 27th. Credited Aaron D. Polhamus for the balance of his account, charged to Remsen & Polhamus, $38.82; and charged Remsen & Polhamus for the balance of A. D. Polhamus' account, $38.82. Remsen & Polhamus have paid me cash, to balance their account, $20.77. 28th. Sold James C. Smith 30 yds. sheeting, at 10c.; and he has given me his note at 3 months, to balance his account, $28.26. 29th. Hugh Jameson has paid me cash, to balance his account, $21.45. Sold Horatio N. Taft 3 yds. black cassimer, at $2.00, 2½ yds. sheeting, at 10c., 1 spool thread, at 5c.; and he has given me his note at 60 days, to balance his account, for $34.67. 30th. Sold Ephraim B. Price 18 yds. brown factory, at 10c.; and he has given me his note at 4 months, to balance his account, for $35.44. Credited Lucius S. Wood for 6 months' services as clerk, at $20.00. Paid him, cash, $35.74, and given my note at 4 months, to balance his account, for $50.00. Gave Philip G. Almy my note at 30 days, to balance his account, for $42.00. James Rogers has paid me cash, to balance his account, $17.14. Joseph M. Demmon has paid me cash, to balance his account, $80.21.

CASH-BOOK.

PETTY CASH-BOOK.

This book is intended for the cash account, so that by referring to it we may at any time ascertain the amount of cash on hand, and, furthermore, by comparing the amount, as represented by the book, with the amount actually on hand, we may detect any error in expenditure.

This book should be ruled like the Journal, as in the form on the following pages. The word *Cash* should be written in a bold hand at the top of the page, near the centre, with *Dr.* over the left-hand money columns, and *Cr.* over the right.

The receipts of cash should be entered in the debit columns, and the disbursements in the credit columns, and balanced every night. For example, see the opposite page.

This book may be written on the last three or four pages of the Journal.

In order fully to illustrate this account, I have given a memoranda of cash receipts and expenditures for January. In order to make the method perfectly plain to the pupil, I have given on the opposite page the form of entry, as far as Jan'y 7th. The pupil will, after carefully studying the explanation, enter the following memoranda.

MEMORANDA.

Jan. 3d. Invested in business, $2,000; paid expenses to New York, $37; bought merchandise, $1,805; paid freight on merchandise, $124. Bought wood of Westfall, $8.00; paid postage, .37c.; received for merchandise sold this day, $5.84. 5th. Paid for sundries, $1.57; paid for sawing wood, $3.00; paid for cartage, $1.75; received for sales this day, $4.92. 6th. Paid for advertising in *Western Whig*, $3; paid for advertising in Wayne Co. *Herald*, $3.50; paid for postage, .25c.; received for sales of merchandise this day, $10.27.

Cash

1848			Dr.		Cr.	
Jan.	3	To Stock	2,000	00		
		By Expenses to N. York			37	00
		" Merch. of Sund. Persons			1,805	00
		" Freight on Merchandise			124	00
		" Balance on hand			34	00
			2,000	00	2,000	00
	4	To Balance brought down	34	00		
		By Wood of Westfall			8	00
		" Postage				35
		To Merch. Sales this day	5	84		
		By Balance on hand			31	49
			39	84	39	84
	5	To Balance brought down	31	49		
		By Sundries			1	57
		" Sawing Wood			3	00
		" Cartage			1	75
		To Merch. Sales this day	4	92		
		By Balance on hand			30	09
			36	41	36	41
	6	To Balance brought down	30	09		
		By Adv. in Western Argus			3	00
		" do. Wayne Co. Whig			3	50
		" Postage				25
		To Merch. Sales this day	10	27		
		By Balance on hand			33	61
			40	36	40	36

7th. Paid for blank book, $2.75 ; paid for merchandise, $5.86; paid postage, 30c. Received from sales of merchandise this day, $12.18. 8th. Paid for merchandise, $4,74 ; paid express charges, $1.25 ; paid for personal expenses, $2,00 ; paid postage, 20c. Received for merchandise sold this day, $11.74.

January 10th. Paid for personal expenses, $8.00 ; a blank book, 75c. ; errand boy, 6c. ; postage, 15c. Received for merchandise sales this day, $15.74. 11th. Paid for 1 gal. of camphine, 56c. ; parallel rule, 50c. ; merchandise bought of a peddler, $7.50. Received for merchandise sold this day, $9,63. 12th. Paid for postage, 25c.; 1 gross Gillott's pens, $1.25 ; merchandise bought at Rochester, $25.00. Received for merchandise sold this day, $14.55. 13th. Paid for a bottle of red ink, 13c. ; hand-bills, $2.00. Received for merchandise sales this day, $12.64. 14th. Paid for repairing blinds, $2.50 ; wrapping paper, $3.00 ; postage, 10c. ; envelopes, 12c. ; wafers, 10c. Received for merchandise sold this day, $10.13. 15th. Paid for express charges, $1.50 ; postage, 15c. Received for merchandise sold this day, $7.96. 17th. Paid for cartage, 25c. ; for hardware bought of J. M. French & Co., $17.50 ; postage, 20c. Received of Miss Mary Emmonds, on account, $2.00. Merchandise sold this day, $16.74. 18th. Paid for postage, 5c. ; bill paper, 75c. Received for merchandise sold this day, $8.63. 19th. Paid for the use of a horse and buggy to Canandaigua, $1.50 ; expenses, 75c. Received for merchandise sold this day, $11.92. 20th. Paid for one cord of wood, $2.25 ; postage, 20c. ; errand boy, 6c. ; cartage, 25c. Received for merchandise sold this day, $17.04. 21st. Paid for advertising in the "Whig," $1.00 ; sawing wood, 75c. ; postage, 5c. ; a lot of bed cords, $5.00. Received for merchandise sold this day, $6.34. 22d. Paid for camphene lamp wicks, 31c. ; postage, 15c. ; ½ ream of letter paper, $2.00. Received for merchandise sold this day, $13.57. 24th. Paid for one gallon of camphene, 56c.; postage, 25c.; ink-stand, 50c. ; cartage, 25c. Received for merchandise sold this day, $15.32. 25th. Paid for 1,000 business cards, $3.00 ; one ream foolscap paper, $3.50 ; one doz. pass-books, $1.00. Received for merchandise sold this day, $9.44. 26th. Paid for making store shelves, $2.50; postage, 5c. Received for merchandise sold this day, $11.88. 27th. Paid for a camphene lamp, 4.00 ; express charges, 50c.; merchandise, $14.13; cartage, 25c. Received for merchandise sold this day, $14.23. 28th. Paid for postage, 15c.; a tin wash dish, 31c. Received for merchandise sold this day, $8.49. 29th. Paid for two doz. whips, $15.00; a new stove for the store, $4.50; fixing the pipe, 50c. Received for merchandise sold this day, $15.94. 31st. Paid for store rent, $25.00; postage, 10c.; four doz. brooms, $8.00; cartage, 25c.; errand boy, 6c. Received for merchandise sold this day, $18.63.

NOTE.—It is often difficult to make pupils understand the propriety of making Cash debit when it is received, and credit when it is paid away. This difficulty may be obviated by explaining to them the original meaning of the word *Cash.* The word originally signified *Chest*, or a place where money was kept, instead of money itself. Now, if I placed all the money I received in a certain box, I could at any time tell by my books how much there was in it, if I made the box Dr. for all sums put into it, and Cr. for all sums taken out. Just so with Cash. Whenever I receive money, I put it in some place, and calling this place Cash, make it Dr. for the amount placed there, the same as I would a person, if I placed the money in his hands for safe keeping. And so, whenever I take out any money from the place where I keep it, and pay it away, I give Cash credit for it. The difference, then, between the Dr. and Cr. sides of the Cash account thus kept, shows how much money I have on hand. On the next page will be found another method of keeping the Cash-Book. Where the page is divided into two equal parts, and the Dr. and Cr. entries separated, and each placed on its appropriate side of the account, it is balanced every night, and the balance brought down. The learner may practice both forms, making use of the same transactions in this as in the preceding form.

Dr. Cash Cr.

1848			$	c	1848			$	c
Jan.	3	To Levi S. Fulton	2,000	00	Jan.	3	By Expenses to New York	37	00
							" Mdse. of Sundry Persons	1,805	00
							" Freight on Merchandise	124	00
							" Balance on hand	34	00
			2,000	00				2,000	00
Jan.	4	To Balance on hand	34	00	Jan.	4	By Wood of Westfall	8	00
		" Mdse. Sales this Day	5	84			" Postage		35
							" Balance on hand	31	49
			39	84				39	84
Jan.	5	To Balance brought down	31	49					

ACCOUNT SALES.

An Account Sales is a statement of goods sold on commission, drawn up by the agent to whom they were consigned, to be transmitted to the person who made the consignment. For example, a person in New York having a quantity of goods to dispose of, sends them to a person in a section of the country where they are likely to find ready sale. The one to whom they are sent is called the agent; the goods, the consignment; and the amount received by the agent for selling, the commission.

FORM OF ACCOUNT SALES.

Account Sales of 3 Boxes Dried Apples and 2 Boxes Dried Peaches, Received by Swiftsure Line Barge Columbus, May 1st, 1848, on acct. of L. S. Fulton, Lyons, N. Y.

1848				
May	25	Sold Hamilton & Co. 3 Boxes Apples		
		369 lbs -- 52 lbs. Tare		
		595 " -- 81 " "		
		581 " -- 85 " "		
		1,545 " -- 218 = 1327 lbs. .04½	59	72
"	30	Sold Miller & Co. 2 Boxes Peaches		
		825 lbs. -- 129 = 696 lbs. .11	76	56
		Charges.	$135	28
"	10	To paid Swiftsure Line Freight $10.94		
"	"	" " Cartage 50c. Insur. 50c. 1.00		
		Our Commission at 2½ per cent. 3.38	15	32
		Balance to Cr. of your Acct.	$119	96
		New York, June 16th, 1848.		
		E. & O. Excepted.		
		Durfee & Emmonds		
		per Wheeler.		

Bills Receivable.

No.	Maker's Name.	Payee's Name.	Amount.		When Given.		Time.	When Due.		Where Payable.	Remarks.
					1848			1848			
1	Moses Austin	Levi S. Fulton	17	61	June	2	30 da.	July	5		
2	Nathan Brittan		38	25	"	10	3 mo.	Sept.	13		
3	James McElwain		33	61	"	16	3 mo.	"	19		
4	Reuben H. Foster		17	77	"	19	3 mo.	"	22		
5	Samuel Moore		16	03	"	"	30 da.	July	22		
6	A. L. Beaumont		62	63	"	21	60 da.	Aug.	23		
7	John M. Holley		40	74	"	23	6 mo.	Dec.	26		
8	James C. Smith		28	26	"	28	3 mo.	Oct.	1		
0	Horatio N. Taft		34	67	"	29	60 da.	Aug.	31		
10	Ephraim B. Price		35	44	"	30	4 mo.	Nov.	2		
			325	01							

Bills Receivable.

All written obligations for the payment of money, which you hold against other individuals, are called Bills Receivable, and should be entered in the Bill-book when taken. By referring to this book the time that notes become due can be ascertained without referring to, or examining your package of notes. Notes received are usually labelled and put away in a safe place, so that constant reference to them would be inconvenient; hence the utility of this book. When the business is so large as to involve many notes, they are usually arranged, so that notes falling due in the same month are in one package—the notes of each month forming a separate package. The page of the book should be divided into twelve spaces, as on the opposite page. Each space should then be labelled as on opposite page. The first note received was that of Moses Austin, dated June 2, 1848, for $17.61, for 30 days. It being the first note, we place its number (1) in first space, the name of maker in the second, the one to whom it is payable in third, the amount in fourth and fifth, the date of note in sixth and seventh, the time it has to run in eighth; then, computing 30 days from June 2d, and adding in the usual three days of grace, we find it becomes due on July 5th, and so enter that date in ninth and tenth spaces. If it had been made payable at any particular place, we would have put the name of that place in the eleventh space, and any particulars as to payment, &c., in the twelfth space. The other notes were entered in same way.

Bills Payable.

No.	Maker's Name.	Payee's Name.	Amount.		When Given.		Time.	When Due.		Where Payable.	Remarks.
					1848			1848			
1	Levi S. Fulton	S. Herrick	64	75	Feb.	25	4 mo.	June	28		P. June 24 64.75
2		H. Bullard	26	75	Mar.	31	30 da.	May	3		P. May 6 26.75
3		J. C. Rumsey	78	63	May	23	3 mo.	Aug.	26		
4		R. O. Fulton	136	00	June	3	4 mo.	Oct.	6		
5		Philip G. Almy	42	00	"	30	30 da.	Aug.	2	B. Geneva.	
6		Lucius S. Wood	50	00	"	"	4 mo.	Nov.	2		
		228.00									

Bills Payable.

All written obligations for the payment of money which you give to other persons are called Bills Payable, and should be entered in this book when given. By an inspection of this, the time when your notes fall due may be ascertained. The pupil will see at once, as he examines this book, that the ruling and method of using is the same as that of Bills Receivable, and it, therefore, needs no further explanation.

Dr. James Bashford in a/c with L. S. Fulton Cr.

1848				$	cts	1848			$	cts
Feb.	7	To 6 Tumblers	.12		72	Feb.	23	By $2\frac{1}{4}$ Bush. D. Plums 2.00	4	50
"	"	" 20 lbs. Ref. Sugar	.14	2	80	"	"	" 5 " D. Apples .75	3	75
"	23	" $33\frac{1}{2}$ " do. do.	.14	4	69	June	30	" Balance	11	82
Mar.	13	" 3 Bbls. Salt	1.12	3	36					
"	"	" 100 lbs. Sugar	$.8\frac{1}{2}$	8	50					
				20	07				20	07
June	30	To Balance		11	82					

Account Current.

An Account Current is a detailed statement of business transactions in the form of Dr. and Cr., as above, and is drawn off from the account of the person in the Journal, or Ledger. It is, in fact, an exact copy of the account in the Ledger, and is drawn off usually every six months, in order that each person may know the exact state of his account with the firm.

Dr. Bank of Geneva

1848				
May	6	To Cash Dep. by L. S. Wood	120	00
"	20	" do. Dep. by L. S. Fulton	50	00
"	27	" do. Dep. by L. S. Fulton	50	00
			220	00
June	1	To Balance brought down	220	00
"	10	" Cash Dep. by L. S. Fulton	400	00
"	21	" do. Dep. by L. S. Wood	50	00
"	24	" do. Dep. by L. S. Wood	125	00
"	29	" do. Dep. by L. S. Fulton	50	00
		$625.00	845	00
July	1	To Balance brought down	782	50

Bank-Book.

This is a book usually given by banks to persons depositing money with them. On the *Dr.* side is entered all sums deposited, with the date and name of the individual by whom deposited: this is done by the receiving clerk.

in a/c with L. S. Fulton Cr.

1848					
May	31	By Balance		220	00
				220	00
June		By Check	$62.50	62	50
		" Balance		782	50
				845	00

At the close of the month, the amount drawn out should be placed on the *Cr.* side, and the book balanced.

The sum total of the deposits for the month should be transferred to the *Dr.*, and the amount checked out during the month to the *Cr.* side of the bank account in the Ledger.

Bill of Purchase.

New York, May 1st, 1848.

Joseph H. Galusha

Bought of A. S. Barnes & Co.

100	Set Fulton & Eastman's	Chirographic Charts	at	$4.00	$400.00
50	Doz. do. do.	Writing Books		1.00	50.00
25	" do. do.	Penmanship		1.50	37.50
20	" do. do.	Book-Keeping		5.00	100.00
					$587.50

Received Payment,

A. S. Barnes & Co.

Bill of Purchase

Is a statement of goods bought at one time, containing the items and prices. If paid at the time, it should be receipted and signed, as in the form on the opposite page; but if charged, in the place of *Received Payment*, write *Charged in Account.*

Bills of Purchase, or more properly Invoices, should be carefully examined, folded of a uniform width, and filed away; and as merchants generally purchase goods periodically, the date of purchase may be written on the band enclosing them. On the first day of January in each year, or at the time of balancing the books, the Invoices for the past year should be put into one package, and the year in which the purchases were made written on the band enclosing them.

All orders should be filed away in monthly packages, with the month written on the band enclosing them, so that when settling with an individual whom you have charged with goods per order, if he dispute your book you can immediately refer to the ordér.

Care should be taken to have all papers, intended to be filed away, folded of a uniform width, for the simple reason that they thus form neater packages.

BILL OF BOOK ACCOUNT.

Joseph M. Demmon

To Levi S. Fulton *Dr.*

1848.				
Jan. 4, To	230 Yds. Brown Sheeting	at	.08	$18.40
" " "	48 " Red Flannel		.38	18.24
" " "	3 Doz. Coats' Spool Thread		.48	1.44
" 31, "	170 lbs. Sugar		.10	17.00
Feb. 29, "	19 Yds. Canton Flannel		.40	7.60
" " "	33 " Shirting		.10½	3.47
Mar. 30, "	128 lbs. Coffee		.09½	12.16
				$78.31

Lyons, May 1st, 1848.

Received Payment,

Levi S. Fulton.

Bill of Account

Is an accurate statement of an individual account, copied from the Day-book, containing a list of the items, the prices, and the date of each purchase. It is sometimes drawn off by the merchant, and sent to the customer, and often at his request. If paid, it should be receipted and signed by the merchant, as in form on opposite page.

Note.—The teacher should enforce these principles and make the pupil proficient by directing him to draw up specimens of the different accounts, &c., that have been explained.

GENERAL QUESTIONS.

What is Book-keeping? How many forms have been given in single entry? Explain Form 1st? Form 2d? Form 3d? What is the Cash-book? What is its use? What does the balance in the Cash-book show? What is the word Cash derived from? How many forms of ruling the Cash-book are there? How often should it be balanced? What should be entered in the debit column of Cash-book? What in the credit column? What are Bills Receivable? What is a "Bills Receivable-book?" For what is it used? Describe its ruling. What do the numbers in the first column of B. Receivable-book indicate? Name in the second, &c.? What are Bills Payable? Describe the "Bills Payable book."

What is a Bank-book? What is entered on debit side of it? By whom are these entries made? When is the amount drawn out entered? Why is this book used? What is an Account Current? When is it drawn off? What is it for? What is an Account Sales? What is the person called to whom the goods are sent? Describe an Account Sales, its ruling, entries, &c. What is a Bill of Purchase? If paid, what should be done? If the goods are charged, what should be done? What are "Bills of Purchase" more properly called? What should be done with these? What use may be made of them? How can you form neat packages of them? Why should you have the packages neat? Are neatness and precision very necessary in Book-keeping transactions? What is a "Bill of Account?" What is stated in it?

PART SECOND.

DOUBLE ENTRY BOOK-KEEPING.

DOUBLE ENTRY.

THIS term is derived from the fact that every business transaction recorded in the Day-Book is entered twice in the Ledger—once on the debtor and once on the creditor side.

DEBTOR AND CREDITOR.

These terms are correlative, the one implies and involves the other. Wherever there is a debtor there must necessarily be a creditor of an equal amount; and wherever there is a creditor there must be a debtor, &c.

APPLICATION OF DEBTOR AND CREDITOR.

In *single entry* these terms are (with the exception of cash) only applied to *persons*, but in *double entry* they are applied alike to *persons* and *property*, the persons being made debtor for what you have trusted them, and creditor for what they have paid or trusted you; and the property accounts being made debtor for the value or cost of the property, and credit for what it produces when disposed of.

CLASSES OF ACCOUNTS.

There are three classes of accounts in Book-keeping, styled Personal, Real, and Fictitious. Personal accounts are the accounts of the persons with whom the merchant deals; Real accounts are the accounts of his property, and Fictitious accounts are titles invented to represent the merchant and his gains or losses in business.

BOOKS USED.

The principal books used are the Day-book, Journal, and Ledger. The auxiliary books vary according to the nature of the business, and are the Cash-book, Bill-book, Invoice-book, Sales-book, Account-current book, Book of Shipments, Letter-book, Receipt-book, &c., &c.

DEFINITION OF BOOKS.

DAY-BOOK.

This book should contain a concise and comprehensive history of the merchant's business transactions; commencing with an inventory of his effects, and the debts due him, also of the debts due by him to others. After this, his business transactions should be recorded at the time and in the order in which they occur; they should contain the date, the name of the person, the condition of the bargain, and price of the goods. In writing this book every thing should be clearly expressed in as uniform a style as possible, and the use of ambiguous words and phrases carefully avoided.

JOURNAL.

This is a book in which the business transactions recorded in the Day-book are prepared to be entered in the Ledger, by ascertaining the proper debits and credits of each transaction. This process is called *journalizing.*

LEDGER.

This is a book in which a page, or portion of one, is allowed for every account found in the Journal, with the name of the account written over the space so appropriated, to which the accounts are transferred from the Journal and placed under their respective heads. This process is called *posting.*

ALPHABET OR INDEX.

In order that the accounts in the Ledger may be more conveniently referred to, an alphabet or index is made by arranging the names of the accounts alphabetically, and placing opposite the name the number of the page on which the account may be found in the Ledger.

AUXILIARY BOOKS.

A merchant's account may all be kept in the Day-Book, Journal, and Ledger; but in most kinds of business, for the sake of abridging these books, it is found convenient to have other books. These vary in number according to the nature of the business, and are termed auxiliary books, and are as follows:

CASH-BOOK.—For definition and manner of keeping this book, see pages 118 and 119.

BILL-BOOK.—For definition, &c., see page 124.

BANK-BOOK.—For definition, &c., see pages 126 and 127.

ACCOUNT-CURRENT BOOK.—For definition of Account-Current, see page 125. The Account-current book contains simply copies of these accounts.

ACCOUNT-SALES BOOK.—For definition of Account-Sales see page 121. The Account-sales book contains copies of these accounts.

SALES-BOOK.—This is a book in which all sales of goods are entered at the time they are sold. After a purchaser has made his selection of goods they should be entered in this book, from which his bill is copied. His name and the sum total of the sale are transferred to the Day-book.

INVOICE-BOOK.—This is a book in which are copied all bills of goods purchased. It is sometimes made of coarse paper and the original invoices pasted into it.

LETTER-BOOK.—This book contains copies of all business-letters.

DEFINITION AND OBJECT OF ACCOUNTS.

FICTITIOUS ACCOUNTS.

STOCK ACCOUNT represents the merchant, and is made Dr. for what he owes when he commences business, and Cr. for what he carries into business. The difference between the Dr. and Cr. of this account is his net capital.

PROFIT AND LOSS ACCOUNT is kept to show the *gain* or *loss* arising from business, and is made Dr. for all losses and Cr. for all gains. The difference between the Dr. and Cr. is the net gain.

INTEREST ACCOUNT is kept to show the gain or loss on interest. It is made Dr. for all sums paid for interest, and Cr. for all sums received for interest. The difference between the Dr. and Cr. shows the gain or loss on interest.

EXPENSE ACCOUNT is kept to show how much has been paid for store expenses, such as clerk hire, store rent, freight, cartage, porterage, postage, &c. For all such expenses, this account is made Dr.; the Cr. side contains nothing until the Books are balanced.

REAL ACCOUNTS.

MERCHANDISE ACCOUNT. This account is kept to show the gain or loss on goods bought and sold. It is made Dr. for the value of Merchandise on hand commencing business, and for the amount of all subsequent purchases; and Cr. for the amount of all sales. If the Merchandise is all sold, the difference between the Dr. and Cr. will be the gain or loss on Merchandise. If the goods are not all sold, the value of the balance remaining unsold should be placed on the Cr. side, and the difference will then be the gain or loss.

REAL ESTATE ACCOUNT is kept to show the gain or loss on real estate. It is made Dr. for its cost—as purchase-money, repairs, taxes, &c., and Cr. for what it produces, either in rent or sales. If it is not all sold, the value of what remains unsold should be placed on the Cr. side of the account. The difference between the Dr. and Cr. will be the gain or loss on real estate.

SHIPMENT OR CONSIGNMENT ACCOUNT is kept to show the gain or loss on property consigned by the merchant to some person to sell on his account and risk. It is made Dr. for what the consignment costs him, that is, the value of the goods, freight, insurance, &c., and is made Cr. for the net proceeds of the sales. The difference between the Dr. and Cr. of this account is the gain or loss.

JAMES HOLMES, CONSIGNMENT ACCOUNT, is kept when goods are consigned by him to the merchant to be sold on his account and risk. It is made Dr. for all expenses you incur on account of the consignment, and Cr. for the amount of all sales. The difference between the Dr. and Cr. of this account is the net proceeds, and should be placed to the Cr. of Holmes' personal account.

WHEAT ACCOUNT is kept to show the gain or loss on wheat as a separate branch of business. It is made Dr. for all sums paid for wheat, and Cr. for all sums received for wheat. The Dr. side of this account showing the cost and the Cr. side what it has sold for, the difference between the two sides will of course show the gain or loss on wheat.

CASH ACCOUNT is kept to show the receipts and disbursements of cash. It is made Dr. for all receipts of cash, and Cr. for all disbursements. The difference between the Dr. and Cr. of this account is the amount of cash on hand.

BANK ACCOUNT is kept to show what money is deposited in the bank. It is made Dr. for all sums deposited, and Cr. for all sums drawn out. The difference between the Dr. and Cr. of this account is the sum you have remaining in the bank.

BILLS RECEIVABLE ACCOUNT is kept to show the amount of written obligations which you hold against other persons for the payment of money. It is made Dr. for all such bills when they are received, and Cr. for all that have been redeemed. The difference between the Dr. and Cr. of this account shows the amount of Bills you hold against other persons.

BILLS PAYABLE ACCOUNT is kept to show the amount of written obligations given for the payment of money that have not been redeemed. It is made Dr. for the amount of all such bills when they are redeemed, and Cr. when they are given. The difference between the Dr. and Cr. of this account is the amount of your Bills that remain unpaid.

DIRECTIONS FOR JOURNALIZING.

Journalizing is ascertaining the proper Drs. and Crs. of every business transaction recorded in the Day-Book, and writing them in the Journal. This requires a little thought. Whenever a transaction occurs, the Book-keeper should reflect for a moment, and see what part of the property is affected by that transaction, and then the accounts that represent that property are the accounts to be made Dr. and Cr. Every Dr. must have a corresponding Cr. of equal amount, and every Cr. must have a corresponding Dr. of equal amount. If the transaction takes from one part of your property, and adds to another, the account from which it is taken is made Cr., and the one to which it is added is made Dr. Whenever you buy property, the account representing that property is made Dr. to what you give in payment for it; or, if you buy it on trust, it is Dr. to the person that trusted you: and when you sell that property, it is made Cr. by what you receive in payment for it, or, if it is sold on credit, it is Cr. by the person trusted.

For example, if you buy Merchandise of Lee, Judson & Lee, on account, $500, Merchandise would be Dr. to Lee, Judson & Lee, $500, and Lee, Judson & Lee Cr. by Merchandise, $500. If you pay them Cash for it, Cash would be Cr.; if your note, Bills Payable would be Cr. Or if you sell Merchandise on account to J. M. Demmon, he would be made Dr. to Merchandise, and Merchandise Cr. by J. M. Demmon. If he paid you Cash, Cash would be Dr.; or gave you his note, Bills Receivable would be Dr. If you give your note to Lee, Judson & Lee on account, they would be made Dr. to Bills Payable, and Bills Payable Cr. by Lee, Judson & Lee. When you redeem that note with cash, Bills Payable would be Dr. to Cash, and Cash Cr. by Bills Payable. If J. M. Demmon gives you his note on account, Bills Receivable would be made Dr. to J. M. Demmon, and J. M. Demmon Cr. by Bills Receivable. When he redeems that note with cash, Cash would be Dr. to Bills Receivable, and Bills Receivable Cr. by Cash.

DIRECTIONS FOR POSTING.

POSTING is transferring the business transactions from the Journal and placing them under their respective heads in the Ledger. Commence with the first transaction recorded in the Journal: suppose, for example, it is Joseph M. Demmon Dr. to Merchandise. You will first turn to Joseph M. Demmon's account in the Ledger, and enter on the Dr. side of his account, To Merchandise (entering the date, journal page, and amount, as directed on page 62), then make a check-mark opposite the name in the Journal, to signify that it has been posted; then turn to the Merchandise Account, and enter on the Cr. side, By Joseph M. Demmon, entering the date, journal page, and amount, and making the check-mark as in the preceding entry. It will be observed, in making an entry in the Ledger, that the account to be debited is made Dr. to the account that is to be credited for the same amount, and the account to be credited is made Cr. by the account debited.

Where there is more than one Dr. or Cr. in the same transaction, the expression used in posting is To or By Sundries.

TO THE PUPIL.

After becoming familiar with the instructions given on the preceding pages, and tracing through the examples on the five following pages, you may copy the Day-Book, commencing on page 148, in your blank Day-Book; then lay aside the printed book, and on a sheet of waste paper journalize the Day-Book entries according to the directions previously given, then compare with the printed Journal to see if you have journalized correctly; then post to the Ledger as above directed, independent of the printed book, and make out your Trial Balance and Balance Sheet as directed on pages 195 and 201.

GENERAL RULE FOR JOURNALIZING.

The thing received, or person trusted is made Dr. "To" the thing parted with, or person who trusts you; and the thing parted with, or person who trusts you, is made Cr. "By" the thing received, or person trusted.

Profit and Loss is made Dr. for all losses, and Cr. for all gains. Every Dr. must have a Cr. of equal amount, and every Cr. must have a Dr. of equal amount.

EXERCISES IN JOURNALIZING.

Transactions.	*Journalized.*
Sold D. W. Clark, on acct., mdse., $200.	D. W. Clark, Dr., $200. Mdse., Cr., $200.
Bot. of D. W. Clark, on acct., mdse., $200.	Mdse., Dr., $200. D. W. Clark, Cr. $200.
D. W. Clark has paid me cash, on acct., $200.	Cash, Dr., $200. D. W. Clark, Cr., $200.
Paid D. W. Clark cash, on acct., $200.	D. W. Clark, Dr., $200. Cash, Cr., $200.
Sold W. W. Hart, on his note, 30 days, mdse., $175.	Bills Receivable, Dr., $175. Mdse., Cr., $175.
Bot. of W. W. Hart, on my note, 60 days, mdse., $250.	Mdse., Dr., $250. Bills Payable, Cr., $250.
W. W. Hart has paid his note, in cash, $175.	Cash, Dr., $175. Bills Receivable, Cr., $175.
Paid my note to W. W. Hart, in cash, $250.	Bills Payable, Dr., $250. Cash, Cr., $250.
Sold J. H. Holmes mdse., $450. Received in payment his note for $250, and cash for the balance, $200.	Bills Receivable, Dr., $250. Cash, Dr., $200. Mdse., Cr., $450.
Bot. of J. H. Holmes mdse., $500. Gave in payment my note for $250, and cash for the balance, $250.	Mdse., Dr., $500. Bills Payable, Cr., $250. Cash, Cr., $250.
Exchanged the above notes with Holmes, $250.	Bills Payable, Dr., $250. Bills Receivable, Cr., $250.
Bot. of J. Dunning his house and lot on Spring-street, $2,000. Gave in payment cash, $1,000, mdse., $500, and my note for the balance, $500.	Real Estate, Dr., $2,000. Cash, Cr., $1,000. Mdse., Cr., $500. Bills payable, Cr., $500.
Sold my house and lot on Spring-street for $2,500. Received in payment S. S. Clark's note, 3 months, $1,000, cash $1,000, and mdse. for the balance, $500.	Bills Receivable, Dr., $1,000. Cash, Dr., $1,000. Mdse., Dr., $500. Real Estate, Cr., $2,500.
The Commercial Bank has discounted S. S. Clark's note for $1,000. Discount, $17.50; cash received, $982.50.	Cash, Dr., $982.50. Interest, Dr., $17.50. Bills Receivable, Cr., $1,000.

Transactions.	*Journalized.*
Holmes & Co., New York, consigned an invoice of goods to me, to be sold on their account, $575. I have paid for freight and charges, in cash, $34.	Holmes & Co.'s consignment, Dr., $34. Cash, Cr., $34.
I have consigned goods to Holmes & Co., New York, to be sold on my account, invoiced $645. Paid freight and cartage on do. in cash, $36.50, and gave my note for insurance on do., $19.35.	Consignment to New York, Dr., $700.85. Mdse., Cr., $645. Cash, Cr., $36.50. Bills Receivable, Cr., $19,35.
Sold Holmes & Co.'s goods for $650. Received in payment P. Almy's note for $300, and cash for balance, $350.	Bills Receivable, Dr., $300. Cash, Dr., $350. Holmes & Co.'s consignment, Cr., $650.
Received an account sales of goods consigned to Holmes & Co., New York. Net proceeds amount to $716.	Holmes & Co., Dr., $716. Consignment to New York, Cr., $716.
P. Almy has paid his note, with interest. Note, $300; interest, $5.25—$305.25.	Cash, Dr., $305.25. Bills Receivable, Cr., $300. Interest, Cr., $5.25.
Holmes & Co., New York, have remitted me a Bill of Exchange on James Anderson, for $716.	Bills Receivable, Dr., $716. Holmes & Co., Cr., $716.
Bot. of J. Jones & Co., for cash, a draft on New York for $583.50, at a premium of ½ of 1 per cent., $2.92, which I have remitted to Holmes & Co., New York.	Holmes & Co., Dr., $583.50. Interest, Dr., $2.92. Cash, Cr., $586.42.
Dean Tisdale has made a draft on me at 30 days' sight, which I have accepted, for $125.	Dean Tisdale, Dr., $125. Bills Payable, Cr., $125.
Paid D. Tisdale's draft on me as follows: in merchandise, $75, and gave him an order on W. W. Hart for $50.	Bills Payable, Dr., $125. Mdse., Cr., $75. W. W. Hart, Cr., $50.
John Doe has failed, and I have sold the note I held against him, of $250, for $100. Received in payment cash.	Cash, Dr., $100. Profit and Loss, Dr., $150. Bills Receivable, Cr., $250.
Bot. a quantity of broadcloth, in company with B. Hartford, $250. Paid cash for my half, $125.	Mdse. Co. A, Dr., $125. Cash, Cr., $125.
Bot. of W. W. Ely, for cash, 100 bbls. of flour for $650, which I immediately sold for $750.	Cash, Dr., $100. Profit and Loss, Cr., $100.
Bot. of F. Cate, for cash, 2,000 lbs. of tallow, for $160, which I immediately sold for $140.	Profit and Loss, Dr., $20. Cash, Cr., $20.
Commenced business with cash, $2,000.	Cash, Dr., $2,000. Stock, Cr.. $2,000.
Commenced business with cash, $1,000. mdse., $1,000, and notes against sundry persons, $500.	Cash, Dr.. $1,000. Mdse., Dr., $1,000. Bills Receivable, Dr., $500. Stock, Cr., $2,500.
Commenced business with cash, $500, mdse., $500, notes against sundry persons, $500, real estate, valued at $1,000; and owe D. Hood, on acct., $250, sundry persons on notes, $500.	Cash, Dr. $500. Mdse., Dr., $500. Bills Receivable, Dr., $500. Real Estate, Dr., $1,000. Stock, Cr., $2,500. Stock, Dr., $750. D. Hood, Cr., $250. Bills Payable, Cr., $500.
Commenced business with cash, $800, mdse., which I bought as follows; of Stewart & Co., on account, $1,700, of Bowen & McNamee, on my note at 60 days, $1,500.	Cash, Dr., $800. Mdse., Dr., $3,200. Stock, Cr., $4,000. Stock, Dr., $3,200. Stewart & Co., Cr., $1,700. Bills Payable, Cr., $1,500.

EXAMPLES.

DAY-BOOK ENTRY.

Lyons, Nov. 1st, 1850.

Sold Isaac H. Jameson on Acct.				
Mdse. per S. B. page 1			500	00
Bot. of J. Hamilton				
Mdse. per I. B. page 1 $800				
Gave in payment my Note at 4 months for	500	00		
Cash for the Balance	300	00	800	00

(JOURNALIZED.)

Lyons, Nov. 1st, 1850.

√	*Isaac H. Jameson Dr.*	500	00		
√	*To Merchandise*			500	00
√	*Merchandise Dr.*	800	00		
√	*To Bills Payable*			500	00
√	*" Cash*			300	00
	The last entry is commonly expressed in the Journal as follows:				
√	*Merchandise Dr. to Sundries*	800	00		
√	*To Bills Payable*			500	00
√	*" Cash*			300	00

The expression "Sundries," as here used, seems to be superfluous, and often confuses the learner, who gets the impression that there should be such an account as "Sundries" in the Ledger. We have, therefore, in the following set of Books, adopted the first method of expressing the Journal entries.

(POSTED.)

Dr. Isaac H. Jameson Cr.

Month.	Day.	Entry.	Journal page.	Dollars.	Cents.	Month.	Day.	Entry.	Journal page.	Dollars.	Cents.
7 1850 Nov.	1	To Merchandise	1	500	00						

Dr. Merchandise Cr.

Month.	Day.	Entry.	Journal page.	Dollars.	Cents.	Month.	Day.	Entry.	Journal page.	Dollars.	Cents.
1850 Nov.	1	To Sundries	1	800	00	1850 Nov.	1	By Isaac H. Jameson	1	500	00

Dr. Bills Payable Cr.

						1850					
						Nov.	1	By Merchandise	1	500	00

Dr. Cash Cr.

						1850					
						Nov.	1	By Merchandise	1	300	00

GENERAL QUESTIONS.

Of what does Part 2d treat? From what is the term Double Entry derived? What kind of terms are "Debtor and Creditor?" What is meant by correlative terms? To what are these terms applied in Single Entry? To what are they applied in Double Entry? What are persons made debtor to? For what are they made creditor? For what are property acounts made debtor? For what, creditor? How many classes of accounts? Name them. What are Personal accounts? What are Fictitious accounts? What are Real accounts? What Books are used? How many principal ones? Name them. Name the auxiliary books.

What should the Day-Book contain? What should it commence with? What should be entered next? In what order? What four things should each entry contain? Name them. What style of writing should be used in this book? What should be avoided? What is the Journal? What accounts are entered in it? What is the use of this book? How are accounts prepared for the Ledger? What is the process of transferring accounts from Day-Book to Journal called? What is the Ledger? How much space is allowed for each account? What is written at the head of the page? How do we transfer accounts from the Journal to this book? What is the process called? What book is used with the Ledger, to enable the book-keeper to find the accounts more rapidly? Describe it.

Could a merchant's account be kept in these three books? Why use auxiliary books? What is the Cash-Book? What is the Bill Book? What is the Bank-Book? What is the Account-Current Book? What is the "Account-Sales Book?" What is the "Sales-Book?" Describe method of using this book? What is the Invoice-Book? What is the Letter-Book? What does the Stock account represent? What is entered on the Debit side of this account? What is entered on the credit side? What does the difference between the Dr. and Cr. of this account show? For what is Profit and Loss account kept? For what is it made Dr.? For what is it made Cr.? What does tne difference between the Dr. and Cr. of this account show? For what is the Interest account kept? For what is it made Dr.? For what is it made Cr.? What does the difference between the Dr. and Cr. of this account show?

For what is the Expense account kept? What does the Dr. side of this account contain? What does the Cr. side of this account contain? When is the entry made on the Cr. side?

What is the Merchandise account? Explain it. What is the Real Estate account? What is the Consignment account? Explain the Consignment account of James Holmes. What is the Wheat account? What is the Cash account? What is the Bank account? What is the Bills Receivable account? What is the Bills Payable account? What is Journalizing? Explain the process. What is Posting? Explain the process.

DAY-BOOK, OR BLOTTER.

DOUBLE ENTRY.

Lyons, Monday, April 2d, 1849.

I commence business with the following effects:				
Merchandise per Inventory	5,214	36		
Cash	2,500	00		
Notes against Sundry Persons	2,300	00		
Benjamin Cone owes me on Acct.	850	00	10,864	36
I owe as follows:				
Lee, Judson & Lee on Acct.	475	50		
Pierce & Wilson " "	287	50	763	00
April 4th.				
Bot. of Suydam, Reed & Co. on my Note at 4 mo.				
Mdse. per I. B. page 1			541	30
Bot. of George W. Betts & Co. on my Note at 6 months				
Mdse. per I. B. page 1			634	96
April 9th.				
Sold Joseph M. Demmon on Account				
Mdse. per S. B. page 1			239	18
April 12th.				
Sold Jameson, Willard & Co. on Note at 6 mo.				
Mdse. per S. B. page 1			201	43
April 14th.				
Sold J. Adams & Son for Cash				
Mdse. per S. B. page 1			221	88

2 Lyons, Monday, April 16th, 1849.

Sold Chas. D. Campbell on Acct. Mdse. per S. B. page 1			602	82
Sold A. I. Hovey for Cash 1 Piece Carpeting 91 Yds. .94			85	54
——April 19th.——				
Bot. of Henry H. Smith on Acct. Mdse. per I. B. page 2			213	14
Sold Jos. M. Demmon on Acct. Mdse. per S. B. page 2			154	46
——April 20th.——				
Dep. Cash in Bank of Geneva			2,000	00
——April 23d——				
Sold Henry B. Holbrook on Acct. Mdse. per S. B. page 3			167	50
——April 25th.——				
Bot. of I. & H. Mirick 400 Bbls. S. F. Flour 5.00			2,000	00
Gave in Payment a Check on Bank of Geneva for	1,000	00		
My Note at 30 days for Balance	1,000	00	2,000	00
——April 26th.——				
Received per Boat C. Demmon, Jones master, from Utica, an Invoice of Wadding Consigned to me by H. H. Smith, to be Sold on his Acct. Amounting per Invoice to $170.80				
Paid Cash for Freight, Cart. &c.			18	75

Lyons, Thursday, April 26th, 1849.[3]

Sold I. C. Dickson on Acct. Mdse. per S. B. page 3			24	75
Shipped per Boat Wm. H. Sisson, Dunn master, and Consigned to Clark & Coleman, New York, to be Sold on my Acct., 400 Bbls. S. F. Flour 5.00	2,000	00		
Paid Cash for Freight, Cart. &c.	205	25	2,205	25
Sold Chas. D. Campbell on Acct.				
1 Bale Ticking 450 Yds. .15	67	50		
1 Case Satinets 600 " .62½	375	00	442	50
April 30th.				
Accepted Lee, Judson & Lee's Draft on me in favor of Tisdale at 10 days sight for			475	50
Sold J. Adams & Son for Cash Mdse. per S. B. page 4			164	50
Cash Sales of Mdse. this month			896	58
Paid Cash for Store Expenses this month per Expense Book			124	00
Deposited Cash in Bank of Geneva			500	00

Lyons, Tuesday, May 1st, 1849.[4]

Bot. of Carleton, Frothingham & Co. on Acct.				
Mdse. per I. B. page 2			496	00
——May 3d.——				
Bot. in Company with R. O. Fulton 5,000 lbs. Wool at .25 $1,250.00 Each to share equally in the Gain or Loss. For conducting the Business I am to receive a Commission of 5 per cent. on all sold.				
Paid Cash for my half	625	00		
Robt. O. Fulton's half	625	00	1,250	00
——May 5th.——				
Sold Jameson, Willard & Co. on Account				
Mdse. per S. B. page 4			227	00
——May 7th.——				
Sold Chas. D. Campbell on Acct.				
2 Bales H. H. Smith's Wadding, 1,200 Yds. 3½			42	00
——May 8th.——				
Sold H. B. Holbrook on Acct.				
Mdse. per S. B. page 5			352	75
——May 10th.——				
Sold Jos. M. Demmon on Acct.				
1 Piece Bro. Cloth 25 Yds. 4.00	100	00		
2 " Cassimere 56 " 2.00	112	00	212	00

5 Lyons, Monday, May 14th, 1849.

Paid in cash Lee, Judson & Lee's Draft on me at 10 days' sight, Accepted 30th April			475	50
Sold E. Hamilton on his Note at 4 months				
Mdse. per S. B. page 6			427	00
May 15th.				
Sold Aaron Erickson for Cash				
5,000 lbs. Co. A's Wool .31			1,550	00
Paid Cash for Sacking, Cart., &c.	5	25		
My Commission	77	50	82	75
May 16th.				
Received of Charles D. Campbell Cash on Acct.			500	00
Sold J. Adams & Son for Cash				
Mdse. per S. B. page 7			250	00
Made up an Acct. Sales Co. A's Wool. Total Sales 1,550.00				
Cost, Charges, &c. 1,332.75				
Net Gain 217.25				
My half of which is	108	62		
Robt. O. Fulton's half is	108	63	217	25
May 18th.				
Bot. of H. J. & M. S. Leach				
200 Bbls. Flour 4.75 950.00				
Gave in Payment a Draft on Benj. Cone for	850	00		
Cash for the Balance	100	00	950	00

Lyons, Monday, May 21st, 1849.

Sold Dewey & Wells for Cash Mdse. per S. B. page 2			22	65
——May 22d.——				
Received of Joseph M. Demmon Cash on Account			100	00
Sold Franklin S. Clarke on Acct. 10 Bbls. S. F. Flour 5.50			55	00
——May 24th.——				
Paid Carleton & Frothingham's Draft on me at sight for			496	00
——May 26th.——				
Received from Clarke & Coleman an Acct. Sales of Flour Consigned to them April 28th Net proceeds $2,775.00 For which they have remitted a Check on Bank of Geneva for			2,775	00
——May 29th.——				
Sold Dean & Burdick for Cash Mdse. per S. B. page 3			103	50
——May 31st.——				
Cash Sales this month amount to			2,000	62
Paid Store Expenses in Cash			250	75
Deposited Cash in Bank of Geneva			1,000	00
Paid Cash for Family Expenses, &c.			124	00
Paid my Note passed to I. & H. Mirick April 23d			1,000	00

7 Lyons, Friday, June 1st, 1849.

Sold Jameson, Willard & Co.		
1 Piece Carpeting 87 Yds. 1.00	87 00	
6 Yds. Oil Cloth .75	4 50	91 50
Sold Henry B. Holbrook on Acct. the remainder of H. H. Smith's Wadding for		175 00
——— June 2d. ———		
Sold Charles Clark for Cash		
190 Bbls. S. F. Flour 5.25		997 50
Made up an Acct. Sales H. H. Smith's Consignment		
Total Sales 217.00		
Charges Posted 18.75		
My Commission at 5 per cent.	10 85	
H. H. Smith's net proceeds	187 40	198 25
——— June 4th. ———		
Sold Chas. D. Campbell on Acct.		
1 Piece Carpeting 96 Yds. 1.00	96 00	
1 " do. 79 " .75	59 25	155 25
Received of Henry R. Holbrook Cash on Account		250 00
——— June 5th. ———		
Paid in Cash my Note passed April 4th to G. W. Betts & Co. at 6 months	616 44	
Discount allowed	18 52	634 96
Paid Isaac C. Dickson Cash		25 00

Lyons, Wednesday, June 8th, 1849.

Bot. of I. & H. Mirick for Cash				
250 Bbls. Flour 5.00 1,250.00				
Which I have sold to Clark &				
Colman, N. Y. at 5.50 1,375.00				
Recd. in Paymt. Mdse. per I. B.	1,000	00		
Their Draft on I. Cole at 10 days	375	00	1,375	00
——June 10th.——				
Sold James H. Gillet on his				
Note at 4 months				
Mdse. per S. B. page 4			480	00
——June 12th.——				
Bot. of I. M. Demmon a House				
and Lot on Broad-st. for 1,600.00				
Gave in payment Cash	200	00		
E. Hamilton's Note Received				
May 14th for	427	00		
Check on Bank of Geneva for	500	00		
The Balance on Account	473	00	1,600	00
——June 15th.——				
Received of Franklin S. Clarke				
Cash to Balance Account			55	00
Henry B. Holbrook has accepted my				
Draft on him at 10 d. sight for			250	00
——June 18th.——				
The Bank of Geneva has Dis-				
counted the Note received from				
I. H. Gillett June 10th at 4 m				
Cash Received	469	27		
Discount allowed	10	73	480	00

9 Lyons, Wednesday, June 20th, 1849.

Sold H. W. Potter my House and Lot on Broad-st. for $2,000.00				
Received in payment Cash	1,000	00		
" Mdse. per I. B. page 3	1,000	00	2,000	00
——— June 23d. ———				
Bot. at Auction for Cash a quantity of Merchandise for $250.00				
and immediately sold it for 300.00			50	00
——— June 25th. ———				
Samuel Sampson has paid his Note with interest, given March 22d, 1849, at 3 months for	1,000	00		
Interest 3 months and 4 days	18	27	1,018	27
Shipped per Boat Rochester, Holmes master, and Consigned to F. S. Bogue, Albany, 100 Bbls. S. F. Flour, Bot. of H. I. & M. S. Leach on my Note at 30 days 5.50	550	00		
Paid Freight and Cart. in Cash	52	00	602	00
——— June 26th. ———				
Joseph M. Demmon has paid his Note with interest given March 23rd, 1849, at 3 months for	300	00		
Interest 3 months and 3 days	5	43	305	43
——— June 28th. ———				
Henry B. Holbrook has paid my Draft on him, accepted June 15th at 10 days' sight for			250	00

Lyons, Thursday, June 28th, 1849.

Bought of H. H. Smith on Acct. Mdse. per I. B. page 1			173	50
——June 29th.——				
Benjamin Cone has paid his Note with interest, given March 26th, 1849, at 3 months for	1,000	00		
Interest	18	08	1,018	08
——June 30th.——				
Cash Sales this month amount to			1,260	00
Paid Store Expenses in Cash per Expense Book			275	50
Paid Cash for Family Expenses, &c.			98	00
Isaac C. Dickson's Salary 3 months' service as Clerk 50.00			150	00
Memorandum.				
Balance of Merchandise unsold as per Inventory taken June 30th, 1849, amounts to $978.34				

JOURNAL.

DOUBLE ENTRY.

1 Lyons, Monday, April 2d, 1849.

2	Merchandise	5,214	36		
3	Cash	2,500	00		
4	Bills Receivable	2,300	00		
5	Benjamin Cone	850	00		
1	To Stock			10,864	36
1	Stock	763	00		
5	To Lee, Judson & Lee			475	50
6	" Pierce & Wilson			287	50
	April 4th.				
2	Merchandise Dr.	541	30		
6	To Bills Payable			541	30
2	Merchandise Dr.	634	96		
6	To Bills Payable			634	96
	April 9th.				
7	Joseph M. Dimmon Dr.	239	18		
2	To Merchandise			239	18
	April 12th.				
4	Bills Receivable Dr.	201	43		
2	To Merchandise			201	43
	April 14th.				
3	Cash Dr.	221	88		
2	To Merchandise			221	88
	April 16th.				
8	Charles D. Campbell Dr.	602	82		
2	To Merchandise			602	82
		14,068	93	14,068	93

Lyons, Monday, April 16th, 1849.[2]

		Dr.	Dr.	Cr.	Cr.
Cash	Dr.	85	54		
To Merchandise				85	54
——April 19th.——					
Merchandise	Dr.	213	14		
To H. H. Smith				213	14
Joseph M. Demmon	Dr.	154	46		
To Merchandise				154	46
——April 20th.——					
Bank of Geneva	Dr.	2,000	00		
To Cash				2,000	00
——April 23d——					
H. B. Holbrook	Dr.	167	50		
To Merchandise				167	50
——April 25th.——					
Flour	Dr.	2,000	00		
To Bank of Geneva				1,000	00
" Bills Payable				1,000	00
——April 26th.——					
H. H. Smith's Consignment	Dr.	18	75		
To Cash				18	75
J. C. Dickson	Dr.	24	75		
To Merchandise				24	75
——April 27th.——					
Consignment to New York	Dr.	2,205	25		
To Flour				2,000	00
" Cash				205	25
		6,869	39	6,869	39

3 Lyons, Friday, April 27th, 1849.

Account		Dr.		Cr.	
Charles D. Campbell	Dr.	442	50		
To Merchandise				442	50
——April 30th.——					
Lee, Judson & Lee	Dr.	475	50		
To Bills Payable				475	50
Cash	Dr.	164	50		
To Merchandise				164	50
Cash	Dr.	896	58		
To Merchandise				896	58
Expense Account	Dr	124	00		
To Cash				124	00
Bank of Geneva	Dr.	500	00		
To Cash				500	00
		2,603	08	2,603	08

Lyons, Tuesday, May 1st, 1849. 4

Merchandise Dr.	496	00		
To Carleton, Frothingham & Co.			496	00
——May 3d.——				
Merchandise Co. A Dr.	1,250	00		
To Cash			625	00
" Robert O. Fulton			625	00
——May 5th.——				
Jameson, Willard & Co. Dr.	227	00		
To Merchandise			227	00
——May 7th.——				
Charles D. Campbell Dr.	42	00		
To. H. H. Smith's Consigmt.			42	00
——May 8th.——				
H. B. Holbrook Dr.	352	75		
To Merchandise			352	75
——May 10th.——				
Joseph M. Demmon Dr.	212	00		
To Merchandise			212	00
——May 14th.——				
Bills Payable Dr	475	50		
To Cash			475	50
Bills Receivable Dr.	427	00		
To Merchandise			427	00
——May 15th.——				
Cash Dr.	1,550	00		
To Merchandise Co. A			1,550	00
	5,032	25	5,032	25

5 Lyons, Tuesday, May 15th, 1849.

Merchandise Co. A	Dr.	82	75		
To Cash				5	25
" Commission				77	50
—May 16th.—					
Cash	Dr.	500	00		
To Chas. D. Campbell				500	00
Cash	Dr.	250	00		
To Merchandise				250	00
Merchandise Co. A	Dr.	217	25		
To Profit & Loss				108	62
" R. O. Fulton				108	63
—May 18th.—					
Flour	Dr.	950	00		
To Benjamin Cone				850	00
" Cash				100	00
—May 21st.—					
Cash	Dr.	22	65		
To Merchandise				22	65
—May 22d.—					
Cash	Dr.	100	00		
To J. M. Demmon				100	00
Franklin S. Clarke	Dr.	55	00		
To Flour				55	00
		2,177	65	2,177	65

Lyons, Thursday, May 24th, 1849.[6]

Carleton, Frothingham & Co. Dr.	496	00		
To Cash			496	00
——— May 26th. ———				
Cash Dr.	2,775	00		
To Consignmt. N. York			2,775	00
——— May 29th. ———				
Cash Dr.	103	50		
To Merchandise			103	50
——— May 31st. ———				
Cash Dr.	2,000	62		
To Merchandise			2,000	62
Expense Account Dr.	250	75		
To Cash			250	75
Bank of Geneva Dr.	1,000	00		
To Cash			1,000	00
Private Account Dr.	124	00		
To Cash			124	00
Bills Payable Dr.	1,000	00		
To Cash			1,000	00
	7,749	87	7,749	87

7 Lyons, Friday, June 1st, 1849.

Jameson, Willard & Co. Dr.	91	50		
To Merchandise			91	50
H. B. Holbrook Dr.	175	00		
To H. H. Smith's Consignt.			175	00
June 2d.				
Cash Dr.	997	50		
To Flour			997	50
H. H. Smith's Consignment Dr.	198	25		
To Commission			10	85
" H. H. Smith			187	40
June 4th.				
Charles D. Campbell Dr.	155	25		
To Merchandise			155	25
Cash Dr.	250	00		
To H. B. Holbrook			250	00
June 5th.				
Bills Payable Dr.	634	96		
To Cash			616	44
" Interest			18	52
Isaac C. Dickson Dr.	25	00		
To Cash			25	00
	2,517	50	2,517	50

Lyons, Friday, June 8th, 1849.

Account		Dr.		Cr.	
Merchandise	Dr.	1,000	00		
Bills Receivable	"	375	00		
To Cash				1,250	00
" Profit & Loss				125	00
——June 10th.——					
Bills Receivable	Dr.	480	00		
To Merchandise				480	00
——June 12th.——					
Real Estate	Dr.	1,600	00		
To Cash				200	00
" Bills Receivable				427	00
" Bank of Geneva				500	00
" J. M. Demmon				473	00
——June 15th.——					
Cash	Dr.	55	00		
To Franklin S. Clarke				55	00
Bills Receivable	Dr.	250	00		
To H. B. Holbrook				250	00
——June 18th.——					
Cash	Dr.	469	27		
Interest	"	10	73		
To Bills Receivable				480	00
——June 20th.——					
Cash	Dr.	1,000	00		
Merchandise	"	1,000	00		
To Real Estate				2,000	00
		6,240	00	6,240	00

9 Lyons, Saturday, June 23d, 1849.

Cash	Dr.	50	00		
To Profit & Loss				50	00
June 25th.					
Cash	Dr.	1,018	27		
To Bills Receivable				1,000	00
" Interest				18	27
Consignment to Albany	Dr.	602	00		
To Bills Payable				550	00
" Cash				52	00
June 26th.					
Cash	Dr.	305	43		
To Bills Receivable				300	00
" Interest				5	43
June 28th.					
Cash	Dr.	250	00		
To Bills Receivable				250	00
Merchandise	Dr.	173	50		
To H. H. Smith				173	50
June 29th.					
Cash	Dr.	1,018	08		
To Bills Receivable				1,000	00
" Interest				18	08
June 30th.					
Cash	Dr.	1,260	00		
To Merchandise				1,260	00
		4,677	28	4,677	28

Lyons, Saturday, June 30th, 1849. 10

Expense Account	Dr.	275	50		
To Cash				275	50
Private Account	Dr.	98	00		
To Cash				98	00
Expense Account	Dr.	150	00		
To Isaac C. Dickson				150	00
		523	50	523	50

INDEX TO THE LEDGER.

DOUBLE ENTRY.

M	
Merchandise	2
Merchandise Co. A	13

P	
Pierce & Wilson	6
Profit & Loss	15
Private Account	16

R	
Real Estate	17

S	
Stock	1
Smith, H. H.	8
Smith, H. H.'s Consignt.	10

T	

U

V

W

X

Y

LEDGER.

DOUBLE ENTRY.

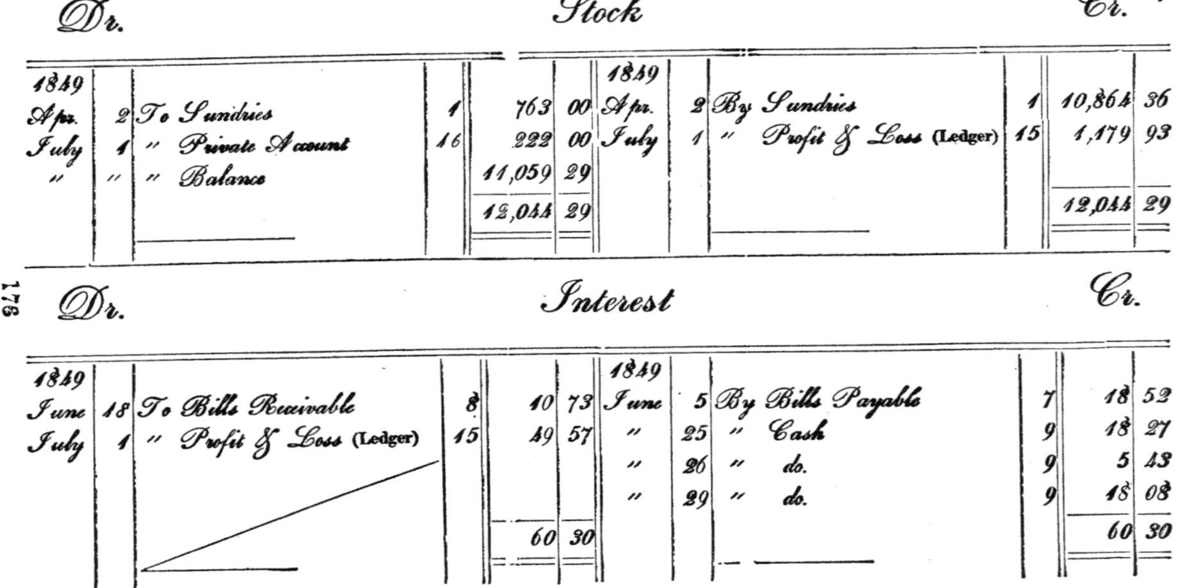

Stock

Dr. | Cr. 1

1849						1849					
Apr.	2	To Sundries	1	763	00	Apr.	2	By Sundries	1	10,864	36
July	1	" Private Account	16	222	00	July	1	" Profit & Loss (Ledger)	15	1,179	93
"	"	" Balance		11,059	29						
				12,044	29					12,044	29

Interest

Dr. | Cr.

1849						1849					
June	18	To Bills Receivable	8	10	73	June	5	By Bills Payable	7	18	52
July	1	" Profit & Loss (Ledger)	15	49	57	"	25	" Cash	9	18	27
						"	26	" do.	9	5	43
						"	29	" do.	9	18	08
				60	30					60	30

Dr. Merchandise Cr.

1849						1849					
Apr.	2	To Stock	1	5,214	36	Apr.	9	By J. M. Demmon	1	239	18
"	4	" B. Payable	1	541	30	"	12	" B. Receivable	1	201	43
"	"	" do.	1	634	96	"	14	" Cash	1	221	88
"	19	" H. H. Smith	2	213	14	"	16	" C. D. Campbell	1	602	82
May	1	" Carleton, F. & Co.	4	496	00	"	"	" Cash	2	85	54
						"	19	" J. M. Demmon	2	154	46
						"	23	" H. B. Holbrook	2	167	50
						"	26	" J. C. Dickson	2	24	75
						"	27	" C. D. Campbell	3	442	50
						"	30	" Cash	3	164	50
						"	"	" Cash	3	896	58
						May	5	" Jameson, Wm. & Co.	4	227	00
						"	8	" H. B. Holbrook	4	352	75
						"	10	" J. M. Demmon	4	212	00
								" Bal. carried to page 18		3,106	87
				7,099	76					7,099	76

Dr.				Cash							Cr. 3
1849						1849					
Apr.	2	To Stock	1	2,500	00	Apr.	20	By Bank of Geneva	2	2,000	00
"	14	" Merchandise	1	231	88	"	26	" H. H. Smith's Consgt.	2	18	75
"	16	" do.	2	85	54	"	27	" Consignmt. to N. York	2	205	25
"	30	" do.	3	164	50	"	30	" Expense Account	3	124	00
"	"	" do.	3	896	58	"	"	" Bank of Geneva	3	500	00
May	15	" do. Co. A	4	1,550	00	May	1	" Merchandise Co. A	4	625	00
"	16	" C. D. Campbell	5	500	00	"	14	" Bills Payable	4	475	50
"	"	" Merchandise	5	250	00	"	15	" Merchandise Co. A	5	5	25
"	21	" do.	5	22	65	"	18	" Flour	5	100	00
"	22	" J. M. Demmon	5	100	00	"	24	" Carleton F. & Co.	6	496	00
"	26	" Consignt. to N. York	6	2,775	00	"	31	" Expense Account	6	250	75
"	29	" Merchandise	6	103	50	"	"	" Bank of Geneva	6	1,000	00
"	31	" do.	6	2,000	62	"	"	" Private Account	6	124	00
						"	"	" Bills Payable	6	1,000	00
								Balance carried to page 19		4,245	77
				11,170	27					11,170	27

Bills Receivable

Dr.						Cr.					
1849						1849					
Apr	2	To Stock	1	2,300	00	June	12	By Real Estate	8	427	00
"	12	" Merchandise	1	201	43	"	18	" Sundries	8	480	00
May	14	" do.	4	427	00	"	25	" Cash	9	1,000	00
June	8	" Sundries	8	375	00	"	26	" do.	9	300	00
"	10	" Merchandise	8	480	00	"	28	" do.	9	250	00
"	15	" H. B. Holbrook	8	250	00	"	29	" do.	9	1,000	00
						July	1	" Balance		576	43
				4,033	43					4,033	43

Dr. Benjamin Cone Cr.

				$	cts					$	cts
1849 April	2	To Stock	1	850	00	1849 May	18	By Flour	5	850	00

Dr. Lee, Judson & Lee Cr.

				$	cts					$	cts
1849 April	30	To Bills Payable	3	475	50	1849 April	2	By Stock	1	475	50

Dr. Pierce & Wilson Cr.

Date			Particulars	Fo.	$	cts	Date		Particulars	Fo.	$	cts
1849							1849					
July	1		To Balance		287	50	Apr.	2	By Stock	1	287	50

Dr. Bills Payable Cr.

Date		Particulars	Fo.	$	cts	Date		Particulars	Fo.	$	cts
1849						1849					
May	14	To Cash	4	475	50	Apr.	4	By Merchandise	1	541	30
"	31	" do.	6	1,000	00	"	"	" do.	1	634	96
June	5	" Sundries	7	634	96	"	25	" Flour	2	1,000	00
July	1	" Balance		1,091	30	"	30	" Lee, Judson & Lee	3	475	50
						June	25	" Consignment Albany	9	550	00
				3,201	76					3,201	76

Dr. Joseph M. Demmon Cr. 7

1849						1849					
Apr.	9	To Merchandise	1	239	18	May	22	By Cash	5	100	00
"	19	" do.	2	154	46	June	12	" Real Estate	8	473	00
May	10	" do.	4	212	00	July	1	" Balance		32	64
				605	64					605	64

8 Dr. **Charles D. Campbell** Cr.

1849				$	cts	1849				$	cts
Apr.	16	To Merchandise	1	602	82	May	16	By Cash	5	500	00
"	27	" do.	3	442	50	July	1	" Balance		742	57
May	7	" H. H. Smith's Consigt.	4	42	00						
June	4	" Merchandise	7	155	25						
				1,242	57					1,242	57

Dr. **H. H. Smith** Cr.

1849				$	cts	1849				$	cts
July	1	To Balance		576	14	Apr.	19	By Merchandise	2	213	14
						June	2	" H. H. Smith's Consgt.	7	189	50
						"	28	" Merchandise	9	173	50
				576	14					576	14

Dr. **Bank of Geneva** Cr. 9

				$	c.					$	c.
1849						1849					
Apr.	20	To Cash	2	2,000	00	Apr.	25	By Flour	2	1,000	00
"	30	" do.	3	500	00	June	12	" Real Estate	8	500	00
May	31	" do.	6	1,000	00	July	1	" Balance		2,000	00
				3,500	00					3,500	00

Dr. **Henry B. Holbrook** Cr.

				$	c.					$	c.
1849						1849					
Apr.	23	To Merchandise	2	167	50	June	4	By Cash	7	250	00
May	8	" do.	4	352	75	"	15	" Bills Receivable	8	250	00
June	1	" H. H Smith's Consigt.	7	175	00	July	1	" Balance		195	25
				695	25					695	25

Dr. Flour Cr.

Date			Fo.	$	cts.	Date			Fo.	$	cts.
1849						1849					
Apr.	25	To Sundries	2	2,000	00	Apr.	27	By Consignment to N. York	2	2,000	00
May	18	" do.	5	950	00	May	22	" Franklin S. Clarke	5	55	00
July	1	" Profit & Loss (Ledger)	15	102	50	June	2	" Cash	7	997	50
				3,052	50					3,052	50

Dr. H. H. Smith's Consignment Cr.

Date			Fo.	$	cts.	Date			Fo.	$	cts.
1849						1849					
Apr.	26	To Cash	2	18	75	May	7	By Charles D. Campbell	4	42	00
June	2	" Sundries	7	198	25	June	1	" H. B. Holbrook	7	175	00
				217	00					217	00

Dr. Isaac C. Dickson Cr. 11

				$	¢					$	¢
1849						1849					
Apr.	26	To Merchandise	2	24	75	June	30	By Expense Account	10	150	00
June	5	" Cash	7	25	00						
July	1	" Balance		100	25						
				150	00					150	00

Dr. Consignment to New York Cr.

				$	¢					$	¢
1849						1849					
Apr.	27	To Sundries	2	2,205	25	May	26	By Cash	5	2,775	00
July	1	" Profit & Loss (Ledger)	15	569	75						
				2,775	00					2,775	00

12 **Dr.** — **Expense Account** — **Cr.**

Date			Fol.	$	cts	Date			Fol.	$	cts
1849						1849					
Apr.	30	To Cash	3	124	00	July	1	By Profit & Loss	15	800	25
May	31	" do.	6	250	75						
June	30	" do.	10	275	50						
"	"	" Isaac C. Dickson	10	150	00						
				800	25					800	25

Dr. — **Carleton, Frothingham & Co.** — **Cr.**

Date			Fol.	$	cts	Date			Fol.	$	cts
1849						1849					
May	24	To Cash	6	496	00	May	1	By Merchandise	4	496	00

Dr. Merchandise Co. A Cr. 13

1849						1849					
May	3	To Sundries	4	1,250	00	May	15	By Cash	4	1,550	00
"	15	" do.	5	82	75						
"	16	" do.	5	217	25						
				1,550	00					1,550	00

Dr. Robert O. Fulton Cr.

1849						1849					
July	1	To Balance		733	63	May	3	By Merchandise Co. A	4	625	00
						"	16	" do. do.	5	108	63
				733	63					733	63

14

Dr. Jameson, Willard & Co. Cr.

Date	Day	Particulars	Fo.	$	cts.	Date	Day	Particulars	Fo.	$	cts.
1849						1849					
May	5	To Merchandise	4	227	00	July	1	By Balance		318	50
June	1	" do.	7	91	50						
				318	50					318	50

Dr. Commission Cr.

Date	Day	Particulars	Fo.	$	cts.	Date	Day	Particulars	Fo.	$	cts.
1849						1849					
July	1	To Profit & Loss (Ledger)	15	86	25	May	15	By Merchandise Co. A	5	77	50
						June	2	" H. H. Smith's Consigt.	7	8	75
				86	25					86	25

Dr. Profit & Loss Cr. 15

1849						1849					
June	30	To Expense Account (Ledger)	12	800	25	May	16	By Merchandise Co. A.	5	108	62
July	1	" Stock	1	1,179	93	June	8	" Sundries	8	125	00
						"	23	" Cash	9	50	00
						"	30	" * Merchandise	13	488	49
						"	"	" * Flour	10	102	50
						"	"	" * Consignment to N. York	11	569	75
						"	"	" * Commission	14	86	25
						"	"	" * Interest	1	49	57
						"	"	" * Real Estate	17	400	00
				1,980	18					1,989	18

(* See Ledger pages)

16 **Dr.** Franklin S. Clarke **Cr.**

Date				$	cts	Date				$	cts
1849 May	22	To Flour	5	55	00	1849 June	15	By Cash	8	55	00

Dr. Private Account **Cr.**

Date				$	cts	Date				$	cts
1849 May	31	To Cash	6	124	00	1849 July	1	By Stock	10	222	00
June	30	" do.	10	98	00						
				222	00					222	00

Dr. Real Estate Cr. 17

1849						1849					
June	12	To Sundries	8	1,600	00	June	20	By Sundries	8	2,000	00
July	1	" Profit & Loss (Ledger)	15	400	00						
				2,000	00					2,000	00

Dr. Consignment to Albany Cr.

1849						1849					
June	25	To Sundries	9	602	00	July	1	By Balance		602	00

Dr. Merchandise Cr.

1849				$	c.	1849				$	c.
		To Bal. bro't from page 2		3,106	87	May	14	By Bills Receivable	4	427	00
June	8	" Sundries	8	1,000	00	"	16	" Cash	5	250	00
"	20	" Real Estate	8	1,000	00	"	21	" do.	5	22	65
"	28	" H. H. Smith	9	173	50	"	29	" do.	6	103	50
July	1	" Profit & Loss (Ledger)	15	488	49	"	31	" do.	6	2,000	62
						June	1	" Jameson Wr. & Co.	7	91	50
						"	4	" C. D. Campbell	7	155	25
						"	10	" B. Receivable	8	480	00
						"	30	" Cash	9	1,260	00
						"	"	" Balance		978	34
				5,768	86					5,768	86

Dr. **Cash** Cr. 19

1849						1849					
June		To Bal. brought from page 3		4,245	77	June	5	By Bills Payable	7	616	44
"	2	" Flour	7	997	50	"	"	" J. C. Dickson	7	25	00
"	4	" H. B. Holbrook	7	250	00	"	8	" Sundries	8	1,250	00
"	15	" Franklin S. Clarke	8	55	00	"	12	" Real Estate	8	200	00
"	18	" Bills Receivable	8	469	27	"	25	" Consignment to Albany	9	52	00
"	20	" Real Estate	8	1,000	00	"	30	" Expense Account	10	275	50
"	23	" Profit and Loss	9	50	00	"	"	" Private Account	10	98	00
"	25	" Sundries	9	1,018	27	July	1	" Balance		8,402	38
"	26	" do.	9	305	43						
"	28	" Bills Receivable	9	250	00						
"	29	" Sundries	9	1,018	08						
"	30	" Merchandise	9	1,260	00						
				10,919	32					10,919	32

TRIAL BALANCE.

The Trial Balance is taken to ascertain whether the Journal entries have been correctly transferred to the Ledger, and may be made as follows:—1st. Rule a sheet of paper with double money columns, and head it "Trial Balance," with Dr. over the left, and Cr. over the right-hand money columns. 2d. Write the names of the Ledger accounts in the open space at the left, and also on the same line in the open space on the right, and, after adding the two sides of each account, place the amount of the Dr. side in the Dr. column, and the Cr. side in the Cr. column opposite the name thus written. 3d. Add the Dr. and Cr. columns of the Trial Balance, and if they foot alike, the books are supposed to be correctly posted. This proof should be taken as often as once a month.

NOTE.—The student must examine carefully the Trial Balance that is found on the two following pages. By noticing how the above rules have been applied he will be able to understand the purpose of this sheet. It is customary, after drawing off or making the "Trial Balance," to label them, and folding them neatly, to place them in a package together, so that they may be readily referred to. In order to familiarize himself with the "Trial Balance," let the pupil draw up a "Trial Balance" of the preceding accounts, and then compare it with the one found on the next page. On the following pages three methods are given—all, however, involving the same principle, and obtaining the same result.

Dr. Trial Balance (1st Method.) Cr. 1

1849						1849					
July	1	Stock	1	763	00	July	1	Stock	1	10,864	36
		Merchandise	2	9,273	26			Merchandise	2	8,783	41
		Cash	3	17,843	82			Cash	3	9,441	44
		Bills Receivable	4	4,033	43			Bills Receivable	4	3,457	00
		Pierce & Wilson	6					Pierce & Wilson	5	287	50
		Bills Payable	6	2,110	46			Bills Payable	6	3,201	76
		J. M. Demmon	7	605	64			J. M. Demmon	7	573	00
		Charles D. Campbell	8	1,242	57			Charles D. Campbell	8	500	00
		H. H. Smith	8					H. H. Smith	8	576	14
		Bank of Geneva	9	3,500	00			Bank of Geneva	9	1,500	00
		H. B. Holbrook	9	695	25			H. B. Holbrook	9	500	00
		Flour	10	2,950	00			Flour	10	3,052	50
		J. C. Dickson	11	49	75			J. C. Dickson	11	150	00
		Consignment to New York	11	2,205	25			Consignment to N. York	11	2,775	00
		Expense Account	12	800	25			Expense Account	12		
		Amount carried up		46,072	68			Amount carried up		45,662	11

Dr. Trial Balance Cr.

1849				$	cts	1849				$	cts
July	1	Amount brought up		46,072	68	July	1	Amount brought up		45,662	11
		Robert O. Fulton	13					Robert O. Fulton	13	733	63
		Jameson, Willard & Co.	14	318	50			Jameson, Willard & Co.	14		
		Commission	14					Commission	14	86	25
		Profit & Loss	15					Profit & Loss	15	283	62
		Private Account	16	222	00			Private Account	16		
		Interest	1	10	73			Interest	1	60	30
		Real Estate	17	1,600	00			Real Estate	17	2,000	00
		Consignment to Albany	17	602	00			Consignment to Albany	17		
				48,825	91					48,825	91

Dr. Trial Balance (2d Method.) Cr.

Date		Account	Folio	$	cts.	Date		Account	Folio	$	cts.
1849						1849					
July	1	Merchandise	2	489	85	July	1	Stock	1	10,101	36
		Cash	3	8,402	38			Pierce & Wilson	6	287	50
		Bills Receivable	4	576	43			Bills Payable	6	1,091	30
		J. M. Demmon	7	32	64			H. H. Smith	8	576	14
		C. D. Campbell	8	742	57			Flour	10	102	50
		Bank of Geneva	9	2,000	00			J. C. Dickson	11	100	25
		H. B. Holbrook	9	195	25			Consignment to N. York	11	569	75
		Expense Account	12	800	25			Robert O. Fulton	13	733	63
		Jameson, Willard & Co.	14	318	50			Commission	14	86	25
		Private Account	16	222	00			Profit & Loss	15	283	62
		Consignment to Albany	17	602	00			Interest	1	49	57
				$14,381	87			Real Estate	17	400	00
										$14,381	87

Dr. Trial Balance (3d Method.*) *Cr.*

				Dr.				Cr.			
1849											
July	1	Stock	1	763				10,101	36	10,864	36
		Merchandise	2	9,273	26	489	85			8,783	41
		Cash	3	17,843	82	8,402	38			9,441	44
		Bills Receivable	4	4,033	43	576	43			3,457	
		Pierce & Wilson	6					287	50	287	50
		Bills Payable	6	2,110	46			1,091	30	3,201	76
		J. M. Demmon	7	605	64	32	64			573	
		Charles D. Campbell	8	1,242	57	742	57			500	
		H. H. Smith	8					576	14	576	14
		Bank of Geneva	9	3,500		2,000				1,500	
		H. B. Holbrook	9	695	25	195	25			500	
		Flour	10	2,950				102	50	3,052	50
		J. C. Dickson	11	49	75			100	25	150	
		Consignment to N. York	11	2,205	25			569	75	2,775	
		Expense Account	12	800	25	800	25				
		Amount carried up		46,072	68	13,239	37	12,828	80	45,662	11

* This method is a combination of the two preceding.

Dr. Trial Balance (Continued.) Cr.

1849				$	¢	$	¢		$	¢	$	¢
July	1	Amount brought up		46,072	68	13,239	37		12,828	80	45,662	11
		R. O. Fulton	13						733	63	733	63
		Jameson, Willard & Co.	14	318	50	318	50					
		Commission	14						86	25	86	25
		Profit & Loss	15						283	62	283	62
		Private Account	16	222		222						
		Interest	1	10	73				49	57	60	30
		Real Estate	17	1,600					400		2,000	
		Consignment to Albany	17	602		602						
				48,825	91	14,381	87		14,381	87	48,825	91

Balance Sheet.

Merchants as often as once, and sometimes twice, a year balance their Ledgers, and make out what is termed a Balance Sheet. This sheet exhibits, in a condensed form, a statement of their mercantile affairs, and forms the materials for opening a new set of books, containing on the Dr. side the debts due them, cash on hand, and the value of merchandise or other property remaining unsold; and on the Cr. side, the amount of their indebtedness to others. The difference between the two sides is of course their net capital.

Directions for Making a Balance Sheet.

1st. Write "Balance Sheet" at the top of a page in the Ledger.

2d. Take an inventory of all property unsold, and make the accounts representing the property Cr. "By Balance" for the value of what remains unsold; then place the name of the account, and the same amount, on the Dr. side of the Balance Sheet.

3d. Ascertain what accounts show a gain or loss on the business, and balance these accounts "To" or "By Profit and Loss" for the difference; then turn to the "Profit and Loss" account, and enter the title of the account, and the amount, if a gain, on the Cr. side, or, if a loss, on the Dr. side of said account.

4th. Balance Private account and Profit and Loss "To" or "By Stock." If the Profit and Loss account shows a gain, carry it to the Cr. side; if a loss, to the Dr. side of the Stock account.

5th. Balance all other accounts, except Stock, "To" or "By Balance." If the Dr. side is the largest, make the account Cr. "By Balance" for the difference, and enter the name of the account, and the amount, on the Dr. side of the Balance Sheet; or if the Cr. side is the largest, make it Dr. "To Balance" for the difference, and enter the name of the account, and the amount, on the Cr. side of the Balance Sheet.

6th. Balance Stock account "To" or "By Balance" for the difference, and, if the operation of balancing is correctly performed, the balance of this account will exactly balance the Balance Sheet.

Dr. Balance Sheet Cr.

1849						1849					
July	2	Merchandise	18	978	34	July	2	Pierce & Wilson	5	287	50
		Cash	19	8,402	38			Bills Payable	5	1,091	30
		Bills Receivable	4	576	43			H. H. Smith	6	576	14
		J. M. Demmon	5	32	64			J. C. Dickson	8	100	25
		Charles D. Campbell	6	742	57			Robert O. Fulton	9	733	63
		Bank of Geneva	6	2,000	00			By Stock	1	11,059	29
		H. B. Holbrook	7	195	25						
		Jameson, Willard & Co.	10	318	50						
		Consignment to Albany	12	602	00						
				13,848	11					13,848	11

INVENTORY-BOOK.

DOUBLE ENTRY.

Inventory of Merchandise, taken April 2d, 1849.

1	Case Ginghams	960	Yds. at	.10		96	00
2	" do.	1,926	" "	.15		288	90
2	" do.	1,842	" "	.12		221	04
1	" Prints	1,000	" "	.08		80	00
2	" do.	2,125	" "	.10		212	50
2	" do.	2,146	" "	.11¼		241	42
4	Bales Cotton Check	2,400	" "	.10		240	00
8	" " Tickings	3,600	" "	.13		468	00
5	" " Drillings	2,250	" "	.09		202	50
3	Cases Satinets	1,800	" "	.55		990	00
2	" Cassimers	800	" "	1.25		1,000	00
4	Ps. Extra F. Bk. do.	162	" "	2.00		324	00
4	" Super. Bk. B. Cloth	100	" "	4.50		450	00
2	" Blue Bk. B. Cloth	50	" "	2.50		125	00
2	" Extra F. Bk. B. Cloth	50	" "	5.50		275	00
						5,214	36

Inventory of Notes.

1	Given by Benjamin Cone March 26th, 1849, at 3 months, due June 26th and 29th, for	1,000	00
1	Given by Samuel Sampson, Mar. 22d, 1849, at 3 months, due June 22d, and 25th, for	1,000	00
1	Given by J. M. Demmon Mar. 23rd, 1849, at 3 months, due June 23d and 6th, for	300	00
		2,300	00

Inventory of Accounts.

Benjamin Cone	850	00

INVOICE-BOOK.

DOUBLE ENTRY.

1 New York, April 4th, 1849.

E Levi S. Fulton

Bot. of Suydam, Reed & Co.

2 Hhds. St. Croix Sugar 2,098 lbs. at .6	125	88
4 " N. O. Molasses 512 galls. " .34	174	08
10 Bags Laguayra Coffee 1,122 lbs. " .7$\frac{1}{4}$	81	35
6 " Java Coffee 675 " " .9	60	75
6 " Pepper 732 " " .6$\frac{1}{4}$	45	75
4 Bbls. Rice 824 " " .3$\frac{1}{2}$	28	84
8 Kegs Ginger 336 " " .7	23	52
Cartage	1	13
	541	30

New York, April 4th, 1849.

E Levi S. Fulton

Bot of Geo. W. Betts & Co.

3 Ps. Super Ing. Carpeting 297 Yds. at .85	252	45
4 " Extra fine do. 416$\frac{1}{2}$ " " .62$\frac{1}{2}$	260	31
2 " do. do. 202 " " .60	121	20
Wrappers	1	00
Recd. Paymt. by Note at 6 mos.	634	96

Geo. W. Betts & Co.

Utica, April 19th, 1849

E Levi S. Fulton

Bot. of H. H. Smith

1 Bale No. 625 800		
1 " " 632 812		
1 " " 653 828		
1 " " 655 839		
3,279 Yds. Sheeting at 6$\frac{1}{2}$	213	14

This is thought sufficient to illustrate the use and method of keeping this Book.

SALES-BOOK.

DOUBLE ENTRY.

1 Lyons, Monday, April 9th, 1849.

					$	cts.
E	Sold Joseph M. Demmon on Acct.					
	2 Ps. Prints	68	Yds. at	.9	6	12
	3 " do.	112	" "	.11¼	12	60
	2 " Ginghams	62	" "	.18	11	16
	1 " do.	29	" "	.12¼	3	55
	1 " S. F. Bk. Cassimer	38	" "	2.12½	80	75
	1 " do. do. B. Cloth	25	" "	5.00	125	00
					239	18
	April 12th.					
E	Sold Jameson, Willard & Co. on Note 6 mo.					
	1 Piece Bk. Cassimer	41	Yds.	2.12½	87	13
	3 " Satinet	72	"	.65	46	80
	1 Bale Ticking	450	"	.15	67	50
					201	43
	April 14th.					
E	Sold John Adams & Son for Cash					
	1 Piece Extra F. Bro. Cloth	25	Yds.	6.00	150	00
	1 " Blue Bk. do.	25	"	2.87½	71	88
					221	88
	April 16th.					
E	Sold Charles D. Campbell on Acct.					
	1 Case Satinets	600	Yds.	.62½	375	00
	2 Ps. Cassimer	49	"	1.50	73	50
	1 " Super F. Bro. Cloth	25	"	5.00	125	00
	2 " Gingham	58	"	.12½	7	25
	1 " do.	27½	"	.18	4	95
	4 " Prints	112	"	.9	10	08
	2 " do.	64	"	.11	7	04
					602	82
E	Sold A. J. Hovey for Cash					
	1 Piece Super Ingn. Carpeting	91	Yds.	.94	85	54

Lyons, Thursday, April 19th, 1849.[2]

E	Sold Joseph M. Demmon on Acct.			
	1 Hhd. N. O. Molasses 120 Galls. at	.38	45	60
	1 " St. C. Sugar 1,114 lbs. "	.7	77	98
	1 Bbl Rice 214 " "	.4	8	56
	1 Bag Java Coffee 108 " "	.10½	11	34
	1 " Laguayra do 122 " "	.9	10	98
			154	46
	April 23d.			
E	Sold Henry B. Holbrook on Acct.			
	1 Piece Bk. Bro. Cloth 25 Yds.	4.50	112	50
	1 " do. Cassimer 27½ "	2.00	55	00
			167	50
	April 28th.			
E	Sold Charles D. Campbell on Acct			
	1 Bale Ticking 450 Yds.	.15	67	50
	1 Case Satinet 600 "	.62½	375	00
			442	50

The foregoing is thought sufficient to illustrate clearly the use and method of keeping the Sales-Book. The letter E in the margin denotes that the transaction has been entered in the Day-Book, and by an examination it will be found that the transactions correspond with the entries made in that Book.

PRACTICAL EXERCISES.

The following is a Memorandum of the business transactions for the month of June, which the learner may record in the Day-Book, journalize, post, take a Trial Balance, balance the Ledger accounts, and make out a Balance Sheet, as in the preceding form.

MEMORANDUM.

JUNE

3d. I have this day commenced business with effects and debts, as shown by the "Balance Sheet" in the preceding form. 5th. Received per boat "Emerald," Collins, master, an invoice of goods shipped by Stewart & Co., pursuant to my order, amounting to $956.00. Paid freight and charges in cash, $46.75. 6th. Sold Henry B. Holbrook merchandise, per S. B., amounting to $56.00. Sold Henry Holmes, for cash, merchandise, amounting, per S. B., to $97.63. 9th. Bot. of Daniel Jones, for cash, merchandise, amounting, per S. B., to $48.96. 12th. Sold Joseph M. Demmon, on account, merchandise, per S. B., $73.19. Received from F. S. Bogue, Albany, an account sales of flour consigned to him, June 25th; net proceeds, $698.00, for which he has remitted me a check on the Bank of Geneva. 14th. Sold David Coleman, for cash, merchandise, per S. B., $139.64; Jameson, Willard & Co., on account, merchandise, per S. B., $158.50. Deposited in the Bank of Geneva, $700.00. 16th. Accepted Stewart & Co.'s draft on me, at 30 days' sight, for $956.00. 19th. Received from Henry B. Holbrook cash, to balance account. Bot., for cash, of J. & H. Mirick, 100 bbls. of flour, at $5.50, which I immediately sold for $6.00 per bbl. 20th. Received per boat

"Swan," H. Denman, master, from N. Y., an invoice of broadcloth, amounting, per invoice, to $316.00, consigned to me by Cromwell, Haight & Co., to be sold on their account; paid freight and charges in cash, $10.00. 21st. Sold Charles D. Campbell merchandise, per S. B., $46.00. Deposited cash in the Geneva Bank, $1,000. 24th. Sold Thomas Collins 32 yds. Cromwell, Haight & Co.'s broadcloth, at $4.50. Received, in payment, his note at 60 days for one-half, and cash for the balance. 28th. Bot. of John H. Holmes his house and lot on Broad street, for $2,000. Gave in payment, cash, $1,000, and my note for the balance. Sold Lewis & Herrick the remainder of Cromwell, Haight & Co.'s broadcloth, for $300.00. Charles D. Campbell has paid me cash to balance his account. 30th. Made up an account sales of Cromwell, Haight & Co.'s consignment; my commission on sales, 5 per cent. Joseph M. Demmon has paid me cash to balance his account. Sold William W. Hart, on his note at 90 days, merchandise, amounting per S. B., to $216. Paid Isaac C. Dixon his salary for one month, $50.00. Store expenses, per Expense-Book, amount to $47.00. Cash sales of merchandise this month, $163.00. Merchandise unsold, per inventory taken this day, amounts to $893.20.

FORM FOR RETAILERS.

Double Entry.

The books necessary for this form are the Day-Book, Journal, Ledger, Petty Cash-Book, Monthly Cash-Book, Merchandise-Book, Bank-Book, Bill-Book, and Expense-Book.

The *Day-Book*, *Journal*, *Ledger*, and *Petty Cash-Book* are the same as those in the "Merchants' Form," Single Entry; also the manner of Journalizing and posting.

Monthly Cash-Book is a book in which the sum total of the receipts and disbursements of cash are entered daily from the Petty Cash-Book; and at posting, the sum total for the month of the debits is transferred to the Dr. side, and the sum total of the credits to the Cr. side of the cash account, in the Ledger.

Merchandise-Book.—This book is kept to show the amount paid and received for Merchandise. Both the Dr. and Cr. sides of this book are ruled with double money columns—for cash purchases and credit purchases; and for cash sales, and credit sales. The amount of merchandise on hand commencing business, also the amount of merchandise purchased, should be entered, with the date, on the Dr. side of this book, "To Cash," "To Bills Payable," or "To Sundries," as the case may be; or if purchased on credit, make it Dr. to the individual of whom it was purchased.

If there should be several purchases on the same day, make it Dr. to "Sundries" for the sum total.

Every night, at the close of business, the amount of the cash sales for the day should be entered in the cash columns, on the Cr. side of this book. At the close of the month, the credit sales for each day should be added in the Day-Book, and entered in the left-hand margin of said book, opposite the date (being careful not to add any that are marked "Returned" in the margin); from thence transferred to the credit columns of the Cr. side of this book. At posting, the sum total of the debits should be transferred to the Dr. side, and the sum total of the credits to the Cr. side of the Merchandise account in the Ledger.

At the time of balancing the books, by taking an inventory of the merchandise unsold, and placing its value to the Cr. side of the Merchandise account in the Ledger, the difference between the two sides of this account will show the gain or loss on merchandise.

Bank-Book.

This is a book usually given by banks to persons depositing money with them. On the Dr. side is entered all sums deposited, with the date and name of the individual by whom deposited. This is done by the receiving clerk. At the close of the month, the amount drawn out should be placed on the Cr. side, and the book balanced.

The sum total of the deposits for the month should be transferred to the Dr., and the amount checked out during the month to the Cr. side of the bank account in the Ledger.

Bills Receivable.

All written obligations for the payment of money, which you hold against other individuals, are called Bills Receivable, and should be entered in this book when taken. At the time of posting the month's transactions, the amount of Bills received during the month should be transferred to the Dr. side of the Bills Receivable account in the Ledger; and the amount of all such bills which have been redeemed should be transferred to the Cr. side of the same account.

Bills Payable.

All written obligations for the payment of money, which you give to other persons, are called Bills Payable, and should be entered in this book when given. At the time of posting the month's transactions, the amount of such bills given should be transferred to the Cr. side of Bills Payable account in the Ledger; and the amount of all such bills which have been redeemed should be transferred to the Dr. side of the same account.

Expense-Book.—This is a book in which a memorandum is kept of all sums paid or incurred by the merchant in conducting his business; such as store rent, clerk hire, freight, cartage, porterage, postage, advertising, fuel, &c., &c. At the close of the month, the sum total of the expenses should be transferred to the Dr. side of the Expense account in the Ledger.

A memorandum of the transactions is given for the months of February and March, which the learner may record in the same manner as the month of January.

As this set of books is to be journalized the same as the "Merchant's Form," Single Entry, we have omitted the Journal entirely, leaving it for the learner to journalize for himself; and if he journalizes and posts correctly, his Ledger will agree with the Ledger in the book.

Note.—The sums to be posted from either the Cash-Book, Merchandise-Book, Bank-Book, Bill-Book, or Expense-Book, may, at the option of the book-keeper, be posted directly to the Ledger, or entered in the Journal, after the Day-Book has been journalized and posted from there to the Ledger.

DAY-BOOK RETAILER'S FORM.

DOUBLE ENTRY.

[1] Rochester, Wednesday, Jan 1st, 1851.

	Levi S. Fulton	Cr.		
	By Merchandise per Inventory		1,598	00
	" Cash		157	18
$16 36	——Thursday, Jan. 2d.——			
	James H. Hooker	Dr.		
	To $2\frac{1}{2}$ Yds. Bro. Cloth	3.00	7	50
	" $1\frac{1}{4}$ " Silk Serge	1.50	1	88
	" 1 Doz. Large Buttons			75
	" $\frac{1}{2}$ " Small do.	.25		13
	Lemuel Potter	Dr.		
	To 3 Yds Cassimer	2.00	6	00
	" Buttons			10
$15 55	——Saturday, Jan. 4th.——			
Paid	James Jameson	Dr		
	To 3 lbs. Sugar	10		30
	Berkley Gillett, Wife	Dr.		
	To 10 Yds. Silk	1.50	15	00
	" 5 Sks. Silk	.05		25
$1 50	——Monday, Jan 6th——			
	Lucius Clark	Dr.		
	To 15 lbs. Sugar	.10	1	50
$4.10	——Wednesday, Jan. 8th——			
	William F. Campbell	Dr.		
	To $16\frac{1}{4}$ lbs. Sugar.	.08	1	30
	" 1 oz. Nutmegs			12
	" 1 " Cloves			13

Rochester, Wednesday, Jan. 8th, 1851.[2]

	Lysander Woodward	Dr.		
	To 1 Bbl. Salt		1	25
	" $16\frac{1}{4}$ lbs. Mackerel	.08	1	30
$14.75	——Thursday, Jan. 9th.——			
	William W. Hart, Wife	Dr.		
	To 10 Yds. M. De Laine	.50	5	00
	" 5 Spools Thread	.05		25
	James H. Hooker	Dr.		
	To 20 lbs. Sugar	.10	2	00
	Eli B. Johnson	Dr.		
	To $1\frac{1}{2}$ Yds. Blk. Bro. Cloth	5.00	7	50
$3.90	——Saturday, Jan. 11th——			
	Henry L. Fulton	Dr.		
	To 10 lbs. Crushed Sugar	.12	1	20
	" 5 " Coffee	.14		70
	" 1 " Tea			75
	" 10 " Candles	$.12\frac{1}{2}$	1	25
$30.35	——Monday, Jan. 13th.——			
	Berkley Gillett	Dr.		
	To Cloth & Trimmings for Over-Coat		15	00
	" 6 Yds. Cassimer	2.00	12	00
	John R. Smith	Dr.		
	To $33\frac{1}{2}$ Yds. Factory	.10	3	35
$15.86	——Tuesday, Jan. 14th.——			
	William F. Campbell	Dr.		
	To 4 Yds. Cassimer	2.00	8	00

[3] Rochester, Tuesday, Jan. 14th, 1851.

	Lucius Clark	Dr.		
	To 3 Yds. Blk. Cassimer	2.50	7	50
	" 3 " Factory	.10		30
	" Buttons			06
$3.00	——Thursday, Jan. 16th.——			
	Lemuel Potter, Wife	Dr.		
	To 8 Yds. M. De Laine	.37½	3	00
$2.56	——Friday, Jan. 17th.——			
	James H. Hooker	Dr.		
	To 32 Yds. Sheeting	.08	2	56
	McKnight & Pardee	Cr.		
	By Merchandise per Invoice		57	00
$1.25	——Monday, Jan. 20th.——			
	William F. Campbell, Wife	Dr.		
	To 1 Pr. Kid Buskins		1	25
Rec'd.	Benjamin Hamilton	Dr.		
	To 1 Table Spread		2	50
$6.80	——Tuesday, Jan. 21st.——			
	Henry L. Fulton, Wife	Dr.		
	To 6 Yds. Alpaca	1.00	6	00
	" 2 " Cambric	.10		20
	" 5 Sks. Silk	.04		20
	" 4 Yds. Jean	.10		40
$5.25	——Thursday, Jan. 23d.——			
	Lysander Woodward, Wife	Dr.		
	To 20 Yds. Curtain Calico	.15	3	00
	" 1 Pr. Kid Gloves			75

Rochester, Thursday, Jan. 23d, 1851.

	Eli B. Johnson, Wife	Dr.		
	To ½ Doz. Linen Hdkfs.	3.00	1	50
$2.08	——Saturday, Jan. 25th.——			
	William W. Hart	Dr.		
	To 10 lbs. Sugar	.09		90
	" 4 " Coffee	.14		56
	" 3 " Candles	.12½		38
	" 4 " Soap	.06		24
$7.55	——Tuesday, Jan. 28th.——			
	Lucius Clark, Wife	Dr.		
	To 32 Yds. Bleached Factory	.12½	4	00
	" 4 " Irish Linen	.75	3	00
	" 6 Spools Thread	.05		30
	" Buttons			25
	McKnight & Pardee	Dr.		
	To Cash		25	00
$2.38	——Wednesday, Jan. 29th.——			
	Levi S. Fulton	Dr.		
	To 10 lbs. Sugar	.10	1	00
	" 1 " Tea			50
	William F. Campbell	Dr.		
	To 2 Galls. Molasses	44		88

5 *Rochester, Thursday, Jan. 30th, 1851.*

$0.88	*Lemuel Potter*	*Dr.*		
	To 1 lb. Tea			75
	" 1 oz. Nutmegs			13
$2.63	————*Friday, Jan. 31st.*————			
	Henry L. Fulton	*Dr.*		
	To 3 Yds. Satinet	.75	2	25
	" 3 " Jean	.12½		38

MEMORANDUM.

FEBRUARY

3d. Sold John R. Smith, per wife, 9 yds. calico, at 12½c., 2 yds. Bishop lawn, at 44c., and 2 linen handkerchiefs, at 31c.; James H. Hooker, 3 yds. gray cloth, at 75c.; and bought of him 28 lbs. butter, at 15c. 4th. Sold Berkley Gillett 50 lbs. sugar, at 7c., and 5 gals. molasses, at 40c. 5th. Sold William F. Campbell, per wife, 10 yds. calico, at 12c.; Henry L. Fulton, 1 pair kid buskins, at $1.25, and 1 pair kid gloves, at 75c. 6th. Sold Lemuel Potter 28 yds. carpeting, at 75c. 8th. Sold William W. Hart 1 satin vest pattern, at $3.25, 1 yd. cambric, at 10c., 1 yd. white do., at 13c., and ½ doz. buttons, at 6c. 10th. Sold Wm. F. Campbell 2½ yds. linen, at $1.00, 10 yds. gingham, at 25c.; and he has paid me cash, $10.00. 11th. Sold Eli B. Johnson, per wife, 10 yds. French merino, at $1.25, 1½ yd. cambric, at 10c., and 6 skeins silk, at 4c.; John R. Smith, 3 yds. black cassimer, at $1.75, and 2½ yds. factory, at 10c. 12th. Sold Henry L. Fulton 2 gals. lamp oil, at $1.00. 14th. Sold Berkley Gillett, per daughter, 6 yds. parametta, at 75c., 1½ yd. cambric, at 10c., and 2 skeins silk, at 4c.; Lucius Clark 15 lbs. nails, at 5c., and 1 gal. lamp oil, at $1.00. 17th. Sold Eli B. Johnson 3½ yds. flannel, at 40c., 2 brooms, at 16c.; and he has paid me cash, $8.00. 18th. Sold John R. Smith 50 lbs. sugar, at 8c., and 2 lbs. Young Hyson tea, at 75c.; Lysander Woodward, 9 yds. gingham, at 25c., 4 lbs. coffee, at 15c., ½ lb. cinnamon, at 44c., and 5 lbs. raisins, at 15c. 19th. Credited Townsend, Hamiton & Co. for merchandise, per inventory, $274,00. Sold James H. Hooker 1 pair rubbers, at $1.13. 21st. Sold William F. Campbell 1 silk pocket handkerchief, at 75c., and 1 cravat, at $1.50. 22d. Sold Lucius Clark 8 yds. gingham, at 31c., and 1½ yd. of cambric, at 10c.; Henry L. Fulton, 5 lbs. pulverized sugar, at 11c. 24th. Sold Lemuel Potter, per wife, 24 yds. calico, at 10c., 5 lbs. batting, at 12½c., thread, at 6c.; and bought of him 5½ lbs. butter, at 16c. 26th. Sold William W. Hart 5½ yds. parametta, at 75c., 4 skeins silk, at 4c.; and he has paid me cash, $7.50. 28th. Sold Levi S. Fulton 4 lbs. candles, at 12½c., 5½ lbs. butter, at 16c., and 1 lb. saleratus, at 8c.; William F. Campbell, per wife, 1 set fine blue tea ware, at $3.50; and bought of him 56 lbs. dried apples, at 5c. Received from McKnight & Pardee merchandise, per invoice, at $74.75; and paid them cash, $50.00. Sold John R. Smith 2 bed cords, at 31c., and 2 yds. table linen, at 75c. Examined.

MARCH

1st. Deposited in Commercial Bank, this day, $500.00. Sold Henry L. Fulton 1 cravat, at $1.50, and 1 pair kid gloves, at $1.00. William F. Campbell has paid me James Cone's note, due June 1st, for $9.50. Samuel Cummings paid me for 3 yds. gray cloth, at 75c. 3d. Sold James H. Hooker, per wife, 6 yds. alpaca, at 75c., 1 yd. cambric, at 10c., and 2 skeins silk, at 4c.; John R. Smith, per wife, 1 yd. black silk, at $1.25, and 1 cord and tassel, at $1.00. 4th. Sold Berkley Gillett 1 pair kid gloves, at $1.00. 6th. Sold Eli B. Johnson 36 yds. shirting, at 12½c., 2½ yds. linen, at $1.00, and 6 spools thread, at 5c. 7th. Sold William F. Campbell 1 whitewash brush, at 75c., and 2 brooms, at 20c.; Lemuel Potter, 15 lbs. sugar, at 8c., 4 lbs coffee, at 15c., 1 lb Young Hyson tea, at 75c., 1 lb. saleratus, at 8c.; and bought of him 10½ lbs. butter, at 15c. 8th. Sold Lucius Clark 16 yds. carpeting, at 75c., and 1 piece binding, at 31c.; Henry L. Fulton, 9 yds. gingham, at 25c., and 1 yd. cambric, at 10c. 10th. Sold John R. Smith 1 satin vest pattern, at $3.00, 1 yd. cambric, at 10c., and 1 yd. white do., at 13c. 13th. Sold William F. Campbell 9 yds. carpeting, at 50c., and 1 piece binding, at 31c.; James H. Hooker, 3 linen handkerchiefs, at 44c., and 1 silk do., at 75c. 14th. Sold Lysander Woodward 9 yds. ticking, at 12½c., thread, at 12c.; and he has given me his note at 30 days, to balance his account, for $11.37. 15th. Sold Berkley Gillett 30 yds. bleached factory, at 12½c., 2 yds. linen, at 75c., and 6 spools thread, at 5c. 18th. Sold Lemuel Potter ½ yd. linen, at $1.00, and 1 pair gloves, at 44c. 20th. Lucius Clark has paid me cash, $10.00. Sold William F. Campbell 1 vest pattern, at 1.75, 1 yd. cambric, at 10c., and ¾ yd. wiggan, at 12c. 21st. Sold Berkley Gillett 9 lbs. sugar, at 10c., 4 lbs. rice, at 6c., and 4 lbs. coffee, at 12½c.; Eli B. Johnson, 1 looking-glass, at $6.00. 24th. Sold James H. Hooker 3½ lbs. soap, at 6c., and 10 lbs. candles, at 12½c. 26th. Sold Henry L. Fulton 24 yds. calico, at 10c., 3 lbs. batting, at 12c., and thread, at 10c.; William W. Hart, 3 yds. ribbon, at 25c., and ¾ yd. silk, at $1.00. 27th. Sold John R. Smith 10 lbs. nails, at 5c., 8 lbs. cod-fish, at 4c.; and he has paid me cash, $15.00. 29th. Sold Lemuel Potter 10 yds. French calico, at 18c.; Berkley Gillett, 10 lbs. crushed sugar, at 11c., and 1 lb. Young Hyson tea, at 75c.; Eli B. Johnson, 1 pair morocco buskins, at $1.13. 31st. Henry L. Fulton has paid me cash, $15.00. Sold William W. Hart 10 yds. curtain calico, at 15c.;. Berkley Gillett, 2 yds. broadcloth, at $4.50, ½ yd. padding, at 38c., ½ yd. silk serge, at $1.13, 2 yds. twist, at 4c.; and he has paid me cash, $20.00. Sold Levi S. Fulton 10 lbs. sugar, at 10c., 9 yds. gingham, at 25c., 5 lbs. raisins, at 15c, 1 oz. nutmegs, at 13c., and 1 oz. cloves, at 12c. Examined.

INDEX AND LEDGER.

DOUBLE ENTRY.

Account	Page
A	
B	
Bills Payable	9
Bills Receivable	9
C	
Clark, Lucius	3
Campbell, Wm. F.	3
Cash	7
Commercial Bank	10
E	
Expense Account	8
F	
Fulton, Levi S.	1
Fulton, Henry L.	5
G	
Gillett, Berkley	2
H	
Hooker, James H.	1
Hart, William W.	4
J	
Johnson, Eli B.	5
M	
McKnight & Pardee	6
Merchandise	7
P	
Potter, Lemuel	2
Profit & Loss	10
R	
S	
Smith, John R.	6
T	
Towns'd, Hamilton & Co.	8
W	
Woodward, Lysander	4

Dr. Levi S. Fulton Cr. 1

1851			$	cts.	1851			$	cts.
Jan.	To Sundries	1	1	50	Jan.	By Sundries	1	1,755	18
Feb.	" do.	8	1	46	Mar.	" Profit & Loss	10	439	42
Mar.	" do.	13	4	25					
"	" Balance	11	2,187	39					
			2,194	60				2,194	60

Dr. James H. Hooker Cr.

1851			$	cts.	1851				$	cts.
Jan.	To Sundries	1	14	82	Feb.	By 28 lbs. Butter	.15	5	4	20
Feb.	" do.	5	3	38	Mar.	" Balance		11	22	21
Mar.	" do.	11	8	21						
			26	41					26	41
Apr.	To Balance Brought Down		22	21						

2 **Dr.** **Lemuel Potter** **Cr.**

Date		Fol.	$	cts	Date		Fol.	$	cts
1851					1851				
Jan.	To Sundries	1	9	98	Feb.	By 5 lbs. Butier	6		88
Feb.	" do.	6	24	09	Mar.	" $10\frac{1}{2}$ " do.	13	1	58
Mar.	" do.	12	5	37	"	" Balance	11	36	98
			39	44				39	44
Apr.	To Balance Brought Down		36	98					

Dr. **Berkley Gillett** **Cr.**

Date		Fol.	$	cts	Date		Fol.	$	cts
1851					1851				
Jan.	To Sundries	2	42	25	Mar.	By Cash	12	20	00
Feb.	" do.	5	10	23	"	" Balance	11	52	35
Mar.	" do	12	19	87					
			72	35				72	35
Apr.	To Balance Brought Down		52	35					

Dr. Lucius Clark Cr.

Date		Particulars	Folio	$	cts	Date	Particulars	Folio	$	cts
1851						1851				
Jan.		To Sundries	2	16	91	Mar.	By Cash	13	10	00
Feb.		" do.	7	4	38	"	" Balance	11	23	60
Mar.		" do.	13	12	31					
				33	60				33	60
Apr.		To Balance Brought Down		23	60					

Dr. Wm. F. Campbell Cr.

Date		Particulars	Folio	$	cts	Date	Particulars	Folio	$	cts
1851						1851				
Jan.		To Sundries	2	11	68	Feb.	By Sundries	6	12	80
Feb.		" do.	6	11	95	Mar.	" Bills Receivable	10	9	50
Mar.		" do.	10	7	90	"	" Balance	11	9	23
				31	53				31	53
Apr.		To Balance Brought Down		9	23					

4 Dr. **Lysander Woodward** Cr.

1851			$	¢	1851			$	¢
Jan.	To Sundries	2	6	30	Mar.	By Note to Balance	13	11	37
Feb.	" do.	8	3	82					
Mar.	" do.	13	1	25					
			11	37				11	37

Dr. **William W. Hart** Cr.

1851			$	¢	1851			$	¢
Jan.	To Sundries	3	7	33	Feb.	By Cash	7	7	50
Feb.	" do.	7	7	83	Mar.	" Balance	11	10	66
Mar.	" do.	13	3	00					
			18	16				18	16
Apr.	To Balance Brought Down		10	66					

Dr. Eli B. Johnson Cr.

Date		Particulars	Fo.	$	cts.	Date		Particulars	Fo.	$	cts.
1851						1851					
Jan.		To Sundries	3	9	00	Feb.		By Cash	7	8	00
Feb.		" do.	7	14	61	Mar.		" Balance	11	30	04
Mar.		" do.	12	14	43						
				38	04					38	04
Apr.		To Balance Brought Down		30	04						

Dr. Henry L. Fulton Cr.

Date		Particulars	Fo.	$	cts.	Date		Particulars	Fo.	$	cts.
1851						1851					
Jan.		To Sundries	3	13	33	Mar.		By Cash	10	15	00
Feb.		" do.	6	4	55	"		" Balance	11	10	59
Mar.		" do.	10	7	71						
				25	59					25	59
Apr.		To Balance Brought Down		10	59						

6 Dr. **John R. Smith** Cr.

Date		Fol.	$	cts.	Date		Fol.	$	cts.
1851					1851				
Jan.	To $33\frac{1}{2}$ Yds. Factory	3	3	35	Mar.	By Cash	11	15	00
Feb.	" Sundries	5	15	75	"	" Balance	11	10	40
Mar.	" do.	11	6	30					
			25	40				25	40
Apr.	To Balance Brought Down		10	40					

Dr. **McKnight & Pardee** Cr.

Date		Fol.	$	cts.	Date		Fol.	$	cts.
1851					1851				
Jan.	To Cash	4	25	00	Jan.	By Merchandise	4	57	00
Feb.	" do.	8	50	00	Feb.	" do.	8	74	75
Mar.	" Balance	11	56	75					
			131	75				131	75
					Apr.	By Balance Brought Down		56	75

Dr. Merchandise Cr.

1851					1851				
Jan.	To Sundries	4	1,736	50	Jan.	By Sundries	4	545	43
Feb.	" do.	8	614	91	Feb.	" do.	8	989	05
Mar.	" do.	14	254	33	Mar.	" do.	14	1,389	73
"	" Profit & Loss	10	786	47	"	" Balance	"	468	00
			3,392	21				3,392	21

Dr. Cash Cr.

1851					1851				
Jan.	To Sundries	4	566	16	Jan.	By Sundries	4	210	66
Feb.	" do.	8	912	50	Feb.	" do.	9	351	80
Mar.	" do.	14	1,359	13	Mar.	" do.	14	2,070	13
					"	" Balance	11	205	20
			2,837	79				2,837	79

8

Dr. Expense Account Cr.

Date			Fol.	$	c	Date		Fol.	$	c
1851						1851				
Jan.	To Sundries		4	104	16	Mar.	By Profit & Loss	10	347	05
Feb.	"	do	9	115	26					
Mar.	"	do.		127	63					
				347	05				347	05

Dr. Townsend, Hamilton & Co. Cr.

Date		Fol.	$	c	Date		Fol.	$	c
1851					1851				
Mar.	To Balance	11	274	00	Feb.	By Merchandise	8	274	00
					Apr.	By Balance Brought Down		274	00

Dr. Bills Payable Cr. 9

1851					1851				
Mar	To Balance	11	181	99	Feb.	By Sundries	9	71	74
					Mar.	" do.	14	110	25
			181	99				181	99
					Apr.	By Balance Brought Down		181	99

Dr. Bills Receivable Cr.

1851					1851				
Mar.	To Sundries	14	20	87	Mar.	By Balance	11	20	87
Apr.	To Balance Brought Down		20	87					

Dr. Commercial Bank Cr.

Date		Particulars	Folio	Dollars	Cents	Date		Particulars	Folio	Dollars	Cents
1851						1851					
Mar.		To Cash	14	1,800	00	Mar.		By Balance	11	1,800	00
Apr.		To Balance Brought Down		1,800	00						

Dr. Profit & Loss Cr.

Date		Particulars	Folio	Dollars	Cents	Date		Particulars	Folio	Dollars	Cents
1851						1851					
Mar.		To Expense Account	8	347	05	Mar.		By Merchandise	4	786	47
"		" Levi S. Fulton	1	439	42						
				786	47					786	47

Dr. Trial Balance* Cr. 11

1851					1851				
Mar.	Levi S. Fulton	1	7	21	Mar.	Levi S. Fulton	1	1,755	18
	James H. Hooker	"	26	41		James H. Hooker	1	4	20
	Lemuel Potter	2	39	44		Lemuel Potter	2	2	46
	Berkley Gillett	"	72	35		Berkley Gillett	2	20	00
	Lucius Clark	3	33	60		Lucius Clark	3	10	00
	William F. Campbell	"	31	53		William F. Campbell	3	22	30
	William W. Hart	4	18	16		William W. Hart	4	7	50
	Eli B. Johnson	5	38	04		Eli B. Johnson	5	8	00
	Henry L. Fulton	"	25	59		Henry L. Fulton	5	15	00
	John R. Smith	6	25	40		John R. Smith	6	15	00
	McKnight & Pardee	"	75	00		McKnight & Pardee	6	131	75
	Merchandise	7	2,605	74		Merchandise	7	2,924	21
	Cash	"	2,837	79		Cash	7	2,632	59
	Expense Account	8	347	05		Expense Account	8		
	Townsend, Hamilton & Co.	"				Townsend, Hamilton & Co	8	274	00
	Amount Forward		6,183	31				7,822	19

* Let the student make the Trial Balance by the three methods.

12 Dr. **Trial Balance*** Cr.

1851					1851				
Mar.	Amount Brought Forward		6,183	31	Mar.	Amount Brought Forward		7,822	19
	Bills Payable	9				Bills Payable	9	181	99
	Bills Receivable	"	20	87		Bills Receivable	9		
	Commercial Bank	10	1,800	00		Commercial Bank	10		
			8,004	18				8,004	18

* Let the student make the Trial Balance by the three methods.

Dr. Balance Sheet Cr.

Date		Account	Folio	$	cts	Date		Account	Folio	$	cts
1851						1851					
Mar.		Merchandise	7	468	00	Mar.		Levi S. Fulton	1	2,187	39
		James H. Hooker	1	22	21			McKnight & Pardee	6	56	75
		Lemuel Potter	2	36	98			Townsend, Hamilton & Co	8	274	00
		Berkley Gillett	2	52	35			Bills Payable	9	181	99
		Lucius Clark	3	23	60						
		William F. Campbell	"	9	23						
		William W. Hart	4	10	66						
		Eli B. Johnson	5	30	04						
		Henry L. Fulton	5	10	59						
		John R. Smith	6	10	40						
		Cash	7	205	20						
		Bills Receivable	9	20	87						
		Commercial Bank	10	1,800	00						
				2,700	13					2,700	13

MONTHLY CASH-BOOK.

The transactions for one month being sufficient to illustrate the manner of keeping the Monthly Cash-Book, we will therefore simply give the sum total of the receipts and disbursements for the remaining months, as follows: Receipts — February, $912.50; March, $1,359.13; disbursements—February, $351.80; March, $2,070.13, which should be posted to the Cash account in the Ledger. For form see next page.

February.

Received for Merchandise Sales	*$887.00*
" on Account	*25.50*
	$912.50

Paid for Merchandise	*$186.54*
" McKnight & Pardee, on Account	*50.00*
" for Expenses	*115.26*
	$351.80

March.

Received for Merchandise Sales	*$1,296.88*
" on Account	*62.25*
	$1,359.13

Paid for Merchandise	*$142.50*
Deposited in Commercial Bank	*1,800.00*
Paid for Store Expenses	*127.63*
	$2,070.13

Dr. **Cash** Cr. 1

1851						1851					
Jan.	1	To	Levi S. Fulton	157	18	Jan.	1	By	Cleaning Store	3	00
"	2	"	Merchandise	11	62	"	2	"	Sundries	4	76
"	3	"	do.	18	95	"	3	"	do.	10	63
"	4	"	do.	29	56	"	4	"	do.	4	66
"	6	"	do.	14	15	"	6	"	do	2	00
"	7	"	do.	27	00	"	7	"	do.	17	50
"	8	"	do.	32	18	"	9	"	Red Ink		13
"	9	"	do.	22	66	"	10	"	Sundries	6	50
"	10	"	do.	10	19	"	11	"	do.		51
"	11	"	do.	15	60	"	13	"	do.	31	05
"	13	"	do.	14	07	"	14	"	Porterage		13
"	14	"	do.	9	14	"	16	"	Sundries	4	25
"	15	"	do.	10	10	"	17	"	Cartage		75
"	16	"	do.	4	36	"	18	"	Sundries		22
"	17	"	do.	17	10	"	21	"	do.	2	56
			Amount Forward	393	86				Amount Forward	88	65

Dr. Cash Cr.

1851			$	c	1851			$	c
Jan.	18	To Amount Brought up	393	86	Jan.	23	By Amount Brought up	88	65
"	"	" Merchandise	25	55	"	"	" Sundries	13	56
"	20	" do.	12	15	"	25	" do.	4	55
"	21	" do.	20	19	"	27	" do.		90
"	22	" do.	8	34	"	28	McKnight & Pardee	25	00
"	23	" do.	9	16	"	29	" Sundries	10	65
"	24	" do.	22	97	"	30	" Porterage		10
"	25	" do.	14	10	"	31	" Sundries	67	25
"	27	" do.	21	17	"	"	" Balance	355	20
"	28	" do.	6	30					
"	29	" do.	4	19					
"	30	" do.	12	56					
"	31	" Sundries	15	62					
		Total Posted to Ledg. p. 7	566	16			Total Posted to Led. p. 7 g	565	86

Merchandise-Book.

The transactions for one month being sufficient to illustrate clearly the manner of keeping the Merchandise-Book, we will therefore merely give the sum total of the purchases and sales the remaining months, as follows: Purchases—February, $614.91; March, $254.33: sales—February, $989.05; March, $1,389.73, which should be posted to the Merchandise account in the Ledger. For form, see next page.

February.

Purchases for Cash	*$186 54*
" on Account	*356.63*
" on Notes	*71.74*
	$614.91

Sales for Cash	*$887.00*
" on Account	*102.05*
	$989.05

March.

Purchases for Cash	*$142,50*
" on Account	*1.58*
" on my Notes	*110.25*
	$254.33

Sales for Cash	*$1,296.88*
" on Account	*92.85*
	$1,389.73

1 Dr. **Merchandise** Cr.

1851		Purchases.	Cash.		Credit.		1851		Sales.	Cash.		Credit.	
Jan.	1	Levi S. Fulton			1,598	00	Jan.	2	Sundries	11	62	16	36
	7	Peddler	14	50				3	do.	18	95		
	13	J. Jones	27	25				4	do.	29	56	15	55
	17	McKnight & Paridee			57	00		6	do.	14	15	1	50
	23	F. S. Clark	12	25				7	do.	27	00		
	25	D. Hoyt	4	00				8	do.	32	18	4	10
	29	J. M. French	9	50				9	do.	22	66	14	75
	31	D. Tisdale	14	00				10	do.	10	19		
								11	do.	15	60	3	90
								13	do.	14	07	30	35
								14	do.	9	14	15	86
								15	do.	10	10		
								16	do.	4	36	3	00
								17	do.	17	10	2	56
								18	do.	25	55		
		Amt. Carried up	81	50	1,655	00			Amt. Carried up	262	23	107	93

1851		Purchases.	Cash.		Credit.		1851		Sales.	Cash.		Credit.	
Jan.		Amt. Brought up	81	50	1,655	00	Jan.	20	Amt. Brought up	262	23	107	93
								"	Sundries	12	15	1	25
								21	do.	20	19	6	80
								22	do.	8	34		
								23	do.	9	16	5	25
								24	do.	22	97		
								25	do.	14	10	2	08
								27	do.	21	17		
								28	do.	6	30	7	55
								29	do.	4	19	2	38
								30	do.	12	56		88
								31	do.	15	32	2	63
			81	50	1,655	00				408	68	136	75
					81	50						408	68
		Total to Ledg. p. 7			1,736	50			Total to Ledg. p. 7			545	43

Expense Account. Dr.

1850				
Jan.	1	To Cleaning Store	3	00
"	2	" Blank Books	4	00
"	"	" Inkstand and Rule		76
"	3	" 1 Gross Pens	1	13
"	"	" Advertising in Daily American	3	00
"	"	" 2 Cords Wood and Sawing	6	50
"	4	" 1 Camphene Lamp and Wicks	4	00
"	"	" 1 Gall. Camphene		56
"	"	" Postage		10
"	6	" 1 Quart Ink		50
"	"	" Bill Paper	1	50
"	7	" Advertising in Daily Advertiser	3	00
"	9	" Bottle Red Ink		13
"	10	" Subscription N. Y. Tribune	5	00
"	"	" 2 Glass Lamps	1	50
"	11	" Postage		20
"	"	" 1 Tin Wash Dish		31
"	13	" Express Charges	1	75
"	"	" Postage		05
"	"	" 1 Duster	2	00
"	14	" Porterage		13
"	16	" Fixing Shelves	1	00
"	"	" Printing 1 Thousand Cards	3	00
"	"	" Blotting Paper		25
"	17	" Cartage		75
"	18	" Postage		10
"	"	" Wafers		12
"	21	" Wrapping Paper	2	00
"	"	" 1 Gallon Camphene		56
"	23	" Porterage		06
		Amount Carried Forward	46	96

Expense Account Dr.[2]

1850				
Jan.	23	To Amount Brought Forward	46	96
"	"	" Cleaning Cellar	1	00
"	"	" Envelopes		25
"	25	" Postage		05
"	"	" Express Charges		50
"	27	" Fixing Blinds		75
"	"	" Sundries		15
"	29	" Livery	1	00
"	"	" Postage		15
"	30	" Porterage		10
"	31	" Blank Book	3	00
"	"	" Cartage		25
"	"	" Store Rent	25	00
"	"	" Clerk Hire	25	00
			104	16

The transactions for one month will sufficiently illustrate the object and manner of keeping this book. The store expenses for February were $115.26, and for March $127.63, which should be posted to the Expense Account in the Ledger.

RULES.

We give some rules that will be found very useful; let the pupil commit them to memory, and make himself proficient in them by solving the example that follows the rules:

Rule 1. To find the gain or loss during business—find the capital at commencing, and the capital at closing business, the difference if the capital at closing be the larger will be the Net Gain; the difference if the capital at commencing be the larger will be the Net Loss.

Rule 2. To find the net capital of the Firm, or of any member of the Firm—add the Net Gain, if there is a gain, to his Net Investment; or if there is a loss, subtract that from the Net Investment.

Rule 3. The difference between the liabilities and resources is the "Present Worth."

Example I.

A merchant invests $2,000 in business. At the close of a month he draws the following information from his books. Cash received, $500; Paid out, $150; A. owes him $40; C. owes him $60; B. has a debit of $200, and a credit of $700; Merchandise on hand, per Inventory, $2,100; Notes Receivable, $600; Notes Payable, $200. Required present worth and Net Gain or Loss.

Let the teacher give to the pupil several examples involving the above principles.

PART THIRD.

BOOKS OF ACCOUNT.

It is a well-established and salutary rule, that a person shall not be permitted to testify for himself, or in other words, manufacture his own testimony. Yet there is an exception to this rule. From the necessity of some cases, the law allows a person to furnish testimony for himself, by admitting his books of account, under certain restrictions, as evidence in his favor.

Such testimony, however, is liable to the strictest scrutiny, and is considered by courts as the most suspicious kind, and as little better than the declarations of the party in his own favor.

To entitle a person's books to be received in evidence, he would have to prove the following facts.

1st. That he had no clerk.

2d. That the books produced are his account-books.

3d. That some of the articles charged have been delivered.

4th. That he keeps fair and honest accounts; and this he must show by those who have dealt and settled with him.

Account-books are not received as evidence of money lent, or money received or expended for the use of another; nor are they evidence of a single charge.

If the entries in a book were made by a clerk, and he be dead, on showing that fact, and proving his handwriting, and that he was a clerk of the party, such entries would be received as evidence.

BILLS OF EXCHANGE.

A Bill of Exchange is an open letter of request, addressed by one person to a second, desiring him to pay a sum of money to a third, or to any other to whom that third person shall order it to be paid; or it may be made payable to bearer.

Bills of Exchange are very useful to business men, who wish to send large sums of money to individuals living at a distance from them. "If A. living in New York, wishes to receive $1,000 which B. in London, owes him, he applies to C., who is going from New York to London, to pay him $1,000, and take his order or draft on B., for that sum, payable at sight. A. receives his debt by transferring it to C., who carries his money across the Atlantic, in the shape of a Bill of Exchange, without any danger or risk in the transportation; and on his arrival at London, he presents the Bill to B. and is paid."

The person who makes the bill is called the *drawer;* he to whom it is addressed, the *drawee;* and when he undertakes to pay the amount, he is then called the *acceptor.* The person to whom it is ordered to be paid is called the *payee;* and if he appoint another to receive the money, that other is called the *endorsee,* as the payee is, with respect to him, the *endorser;* any one who happens for the time to have the legal possession of the bill, is called the *holder* of it.

A bill is either *foreign* or *inland.* It is called foreign when drawn by a person in one state or country, upon one in another state or country; and inland, when both drawer and drawee reside in the same state. These are generally termed drafts.

Foreign bills are usually drawn in sets; that is copies of the bill are made on separate pieces of paper, each part containing a condition that it shall continue payable only so long as the others remain unpaid. Whenever any one of a set is paid, the others are void; for the whole set constitute but one bill. The reason for drawing them in sets is, that in case one part is lost or accidentally destroyed, the other may be received by the drawee.

OF THE REQUISITES OF A BILL.

A Bill of Exchange must always be in writing. It is not necessary that it should be written in ink; it may be in pencil mark. No precise form of words is necessary. It will be sufficient if it contain an order or direction by one person to another, to pay money to a third. It must be for the payment of *money,* and money only; and the sum to be paid must be payable absolutely and at all events, and must not depend upon any circumstance that may, or may not happen; the exact sum also must be inserted. The place where, and on which it is drawn, should, in general, appear upon the face of the bill; there should also be a date, though its omission would not render the bill invalid. The time when bills are payable should be fixed; usually they are drawn payable at a certain time after date or after sight; that is, after acceptance.

It is not essential to the validity of a bill that it be negotiable, or that it contain the words "value received," although in many cases it is highly important that these words be inserted.

OF THE OBLIGATIONS OF PARTIES.

The drawer's undertaking in a Bill of Exchange is, that the drawee, upon due presentment to him, shall accept such bill, and pay the same when due; and that if the drawee do not accept it, or pay it when due, he will pay the amount of the bill to the holder, together with certain damages which the law allows; provided he is duly notified of such non-payment.

It is the payee's duty, if the bill remain in his possession, to present it to the drawee for acceptance and for payment at the proper time and place, and in case the drawee refuse to accept or pay, to give notice without delay to the drawer of such refusal. If the payee endorse the bill, his undertaking, in regard to all subsequent holders, is exactly the same as the drawer's.

The obligations of the endorsee or holder, are the same as those of the payee previous to his endorsing the bill.

The acceptor undertakes, and is bound to pay the bill, according to the tenor of the acceptance, when it becomes due, and upon due presentment thereof. In short, all those who have signed, accepted, or endorsed a bill of exchange, are jointly and severally liable upon it to the holder.

OF TRANSFER.

A bill which does not contain a direction or request to pay to the *order of the payee* or to *the bearer*, is not negotiable or transferable, so as to render the drawer or acceptor liable to the person to whom it is transferred, though the payee would be liable on his endorsing such a bill, and the endorsee could recover against him.

A bill which is made payable *to order*, is transferable only by endorsement; but if payable *to bearer*, it is transferable by mere delivery. Endorsements are of two kinds—*blank*, and *full* or *special* endorsements. A *blank* endorsement is made by the mere signature of the endorser on the back of the bill; and if it be the signature of the payee, its effect is to make the bill thereafter payable to bearer.

An endorsement *in full* expresses in whose favor the endorsement is made. Thus an endorsement in full by A. B. is usually in this form: "Pay C. D. or order," and signed "A. B." Its effect is to make the bill payable to C. D., or his order only.

An endorsee has a right to convert a *blank* endorsement into a *special* one, by writing over the signature the necessary words; and on the other hand he may convert a *special* into a *blank* endorsement by striking out the words that made it an endorsement in *full*.

OF PRESENTMENT FOR ACCEPTANCE.

If a bill be drawn payable at sight, or at a certain period after sight, or after demand, it is absolutely necessary that the holder present it to the drawee for acceptance. For until such presentment there is no right of action against any party; and generally, unless it be made within a reasonable time, the holder loses his remedy against the antecedent parties.

OF ACCEPTANCE.

An Acceptance is an engagement by the drawee to pay the bill when due. It may be general or conditional, and either before or after the bill is drawn. It must be in writing, though no precise form is necessary; any written words clearly denoting an intention to accept the bill are sufficient.

The holder is entitled to require from the drawee an absolute engagement to pay according to the tenor of the bill, unencumbered with any condition or qualification. If the drawee refuse to give the holder a general and unqualified acceptance, he may treat the bill as dishonored.

A bill is said to be honored when it is duly accepted; and when acceptance or payment is refused, it is said to be dishonored

OF PROCEEDINGS ON NON-ACCEPTANCE.

Immediately upon the dishonor of a bill, by the refusal of the drawee to accept it, it is in general the indispensable duty of the holder to have the bill duly protested, and notice of such dishonor and protest given to the antecedent parties to whom he intends to look for indemnity.

The protest is generally drawn up by a notary public; it is a solemn declaration against any loss to be sustained on the part of the holder by the non-acceptance or non-payment of the bill. In respect to inland bills, a protest is not absolutely necessary, although it is usual; notice of their dishonor, however, must be given by the holder to the antecedent parties, in order to make them responsible.

Upon non-acceptance of a bill, if due notice thereof has been given to the antecedent parties, the holder can insist upon immediate payment of the bill from them.

OF PRESENTMENT FOR PAYMENT.

If the bill has been duly accepted, it is the duty of the holder to present it to the acceptor for payment on the very day on which it becomes due; and if the bill was accepted payable at a particular place, the holder is bound to make a demand of payment at that place. For, if the holder neglect to present the bill at such time and place, he cannot recover against the drawer or endorser in case the acceptor refuses payment.

In determining when a bill becomes due, days of grace, as they are called, must be allowed. In this country three days' grace are given on all bills except those payable on demand. Demand of payment must not be made, therefore, until the third day of grace, unless such day be Sunday, Fourth of July, or some other holiday, in which case demand must be made on the second day of grace.

OF PROCEEDINGS ON NON-PAYMENT.

The duties of the holder, upon dishonor of a bill by non-payment, are the same as upon dishonor by non-acceptance. He must make due protest for non-payment, and give due notice of the dishonor to the other parties to the bill; in which case the holder is entitled to a full satisfaction of all damages sustained by him by reason of the dishonor, against such other parties to the bill; but if he neglect to do this, the antecedent parties are discharged from all liability to the holder

OF PAYMENT AND OTHER DISCHARGES.

The acceptor being primarily liable on a bill of exchange, it is evident that a payment by him to the holder discharges all the other parties from liability on the bill, provided the payment is made without knowledge of any infirmity in the title of the holder, and the names of the parties to the bill are not forgeries. Payment by the acceptor should be made at maturity, and not before.

The drawer and endorsers will be discharged from liability by a valid and binding agreement (in which they do not concur) between the holder and acceptor, whereby time is given to the acceptor for the payment of the bill after it is due.

A discharge to the acceptor, we have seen, is a discharge to all the parties to the bill; but a discharge to an indorser is no discharge to the prior endorsers, though it is to the subsequent endorsers.

FORM OF A SET OF BILLS OF EXCHANGE.

Exch. $1,000.

NEW YORK, Jan. 1, 1848.

Thirty days after sight of this, my first of exchange (second and third unpaid), pay to the order of H. B. Williams & Co., one thousand dollars, and place the same to my account.

L. S. F.

To Messrs. Jones & Clark,
New Orleans.

Exch. $1,000.

NEW YORK, Jan. 1, 1848.

Thirty days after sight of this, my second of exchange (first and third unpaid), pay to the order of H. B. Williams & Co. one thousand dollars, and place the same to my account.

L. S. F.

To Messrs. Jones & Clark,
New Orleans.

Exch. $1,000.

NEW YORK, Jan. 1, 1848.

Thirty days after sight of this, my third of exchange (first and second unpaid), pay to the order of H. B. Williams & Co. one thousand dollars, and place the same to my account.

L. S. F.

To Messrs. Jones & Clark,
New Orleans.

FORM OF A DRAFT OR INLAND BILL.

$500.

LYONS, Jan. 1, 1848.

Ten days from sight pay to the order of Nathan Brittan five hundred dollars, value received, and place the same to my account.

L. S. F.

To H. M. Richardson,
Rochester.

PROMISSORY NOTES.

A promissory note is an engagement in writing to pay a certain sum of money mentioned in it to a person named, or to his order, or to such person or bearer.

A note, in its original form of a promise from one person to pay a sum of money to another, bears no particular resemblance to a bill of exchange; but when it is endorsed there is a very great resemblance, for then it is an order by the endorser to the maker of the note, to pay the money to the endorsee. The *endorser* of the note corresponds to the *drawer* of the bill; the *maker* to the *drawee* or *acceptor;* and the *endorsee* to the *payee.* The rights and obligations of these corresponding parties are nearly or quite the same. It will not be necessary, therefore, to repeat all the rules that are applicable to, and govern the parties to a promissory note; we will, however, state the principal ones. And first, of *the requisites of promissory notes.*

No precise form of words is necessary to constitute a valid promissory note. A promise to account for a certain sum, or an acknowledgment of indebtedness for value received, is sufficient.

Like bills of exchange, they must be for the payment of *money* only, and not for the performance of some other act; and the amount to be paid must be fixed and not variable, and must not depend upon any contingency, but must be payable absolutely and at all events.

There should be no uncertainty as to the person by whom or to whom it is payable. Therefore a note payable to A. B., *or* to C. D., is not a valid promissory note.

A note payable to bearer generally, or to the payee or bearer, is transferable by mere delivery; and possession of such a note is *prima facie* proof of title. But if a note be drawn payable to the *order* of the payee, the title will pass only by the endorsement of the payee; and if the endorsement be *in full,* the title passes to the person named therein; but if it be *in blank,* it passes to the holder by delivery merely.

To make a note payable at a particular place, it is not sufficient that there be a memorandum of the place at the bottom or margin thereof, but it must be expressed in the body of the note itself, and form a part thereof.

The words "value received" are not essential to the validity of a promissory note, although they should be inserted.

A note may be made by two or more persons; and in that case may be joint, or joint and several, according to its form. The makers of a joint and several note may be sued upon it either jointly or separately; and if sued separately, a recovery of judgment (without satisfaction) against one will not be a bar to a recovery against another maker. But the makers of a joint note should be sued jointly; for if they are sued separately the action can be defeated by a plea in abatement of the non-joinder of the other maker or makers.

A note signed by two or more persons written thus, "We promise to pay," &c., is a joint note only; otherwise, if the words "jointly and severally" be added. A note written, "I promise to pay," &c., signed by two or more persons, is a joint and several note.

If a person *at the time* a negotiable note is made, write on the back of it, "I guarantee the payment of the within note," he will be treated as a joint and several promiser with the maker thereof, and not as a mere guarantor. But if the endorsement be made at a *subsequent time*, or be a guarantee of *collection* instead of *payment*, the endorser would be considered as a guarantor; a consideration, however, in these last cases, must be expressed; that is, the words "for value received" should be inserted in the endorsement.

If a note be endorsed thus, "For value received," or "For a valuable consideration I guarantee the collection of the within note," the guarantor would not be liable upon it, unless the holder showed a diligent attempt to collect it.

An agreement for a *valid consideration*, extending to a principal the time of payment of a debt, discharges the sureties. But an agreement for delay, made *without consideration*, between the principal debtor and the creditor, will not discharge the surety; nor will negligence of the creditor in calling upon the principal for payment discharge the surety, unless he be damnified by such negligence.

All who have signed or endorsed a note, are jointly and severally liable to the holder.

CONSIDERATION.

A valuable consideration is necessary to support a promissory note. A consideration founded on mere love or affection is not sufficient. Thus, a note drawn as a gift to a son or other relative, or to a friend, cannot be enforced as between the original parties.

A mere moral obligation, though coupled with an express promise, is not sufficient consideration to support a note. A consideration which the law esteems *valuable* must exist, in order to furnish a just foundation for an action.

A note will be void, as between the original parties, if founded upon fraud or duress, or where undue advantage was taken to obtain it of the maker; as, for instance, getting the maker intoxicated for the purpose of obtaining his note.

Illegal consideration also will render a note void; as, when a note is given for the perpetration or concealment of a crime, or for a wager, or whenever the consideration is founded upon a transaction against sound morals, public policy, public rights, or public interests. There are, however, but two cases in which a note is void in the hands of an *innocent endorser* for a *valuable consideration;* and these cases are, when the consideration in the note is money won at a play, or where the note is given for a usurious debt.

ON PRESENTMENT FOR PAYMENT.

The contract of the maker being to pay the note upon due presentment at maturity, in order to charge the endorsers, it is the duty of the holder to demand payment of the maker on the very day on which by law the note becomes due; and unless the demand be so made the holder loses his remedy against the endorsers, although the maker would still be liable. The rules that were given to determine when bills of exchange become due apply as well to notes. Three days' grace are allowed on all notes except those payable on demand, and those in which no time of payment is expressed; on such no days of grace are allowed.

When a note is made payable at any particular place, as, for instance, at a certain bank, due presentment must be made at that place in order to render the endorsers liable in case of non-payment. Notes payable at a particular bank, are generally left with that bank for payment.

If the note is payable generally, without any specification of place, the holder may present it for payment to the maker wherever he may be found; but it is not absolutely necessary that a personal demand be made; a demand at the maker's place of abode or business, is a good demand in some cases. The holder must use reasonable diligence in finding the maker, or his place of abode, or place of business, in order to charge the endorsers. But the maker is liable without such demand.

PROCEEDINGS ON NON-PAYMENT.

No protest is required to be made upon the dishonor of a note; although it is common to protest them for non-payment, especially in commercial towns. But in every case of the dishonor of a note, it is the duty of the holder to give due notice thereof to all the prior parties on the note to whom he means to look for payment; for the holder cannot recover against a party to whom he has failed to give due notice of the dishonor.

OF PAYMENT.

If the maker makes due payment of a note to a *bona fide* holder, it will amount to a complete discharge of all other parties thereon.

But when payment is duly made by an endorser to the holder, such endorser, as a general rule, will retain his right to recover over against all the antecedent parties to the note, until he has received a full indemnity; such payment, however, will discharge all the endorsers subsequent to himself.

INTEREST.

Interest is recoverable on a promissory note in which there is no special agreement to pay interest, from the time when the principal becomes due, or ought to have been paid. A note payable on demand carries no interest till a demand is made, either by suit or otherwise, unless there is an agreement to pay interest. A note not on demand, in which no time of payment is mentioned, draws interest from date.

Whenever there is a special agreement to pay interest, that is, when the words "with use," or "with interest," &c., are contained in the note, it draws interest, of course, according to such agreement or contract.

A note is said to be outlawed in six years from the time it becomes due. The statute requires that all actions founded upon any instrument or contract not under seal, must be commenced within six years next after the cause of action accrued, and not after.

FORMS OF PROMISSORY NOTES.

(1.)

Nine months from date, for value received, I promise to pay H. M. Richardson, or bearer, one hundred dollars with interest.

L. S. FAINSTOCK.

Lyons, Aug. 1, 1848.

(2.)

On the first day of January, 1849, for value received, I promise to pay L. S. Fulton, or order, one hundred dollars.

SAMUEL TOOK.

(3.)

On demand, for value received, I promise to pay H. M. Richardson, or bearer, one hundred and ninety-two dollars and sixty cents.

ALEX. HAMILTON.

Lyons, Jan. 1, 1849.

(4.)

For value received, I promise to pay L. S. Fulton, or order, one hundred and fifty dollars.

JOHN JONES.

Lyons, Aug. 1, 1848.

(5.)

Ninety days after date, for value received, I promise to pay H. M. Richardson, at the Bank of Geneva, one hundred and twenty-five dollars.

S. S. SAMPSON.

Lyons, Aug. 1, 1848.

(6.)

JOINT NOTE.

Three months after date, for value received, we jointly and severally promise to pay to the order of L. S. Fulton, one hundred dollars with interest.

SAMUEL SAMPSON.
JAMES JAMESON.

Lyons, Aug. 1, 1848.

(7.)

DUE-BILL.

Due, Lyons, Jan. 1, 1848, Levi S. Fulton one hundred and forty-seven dollars.

SAMUEL SAMMERS.

Notes Nos. 1, 4, 6, and 7 draw interest from their date; Nos. 2 and 5 from the time of payment mentioned in them; and No. 3 from the time a demand is made.

CHATTEL NOTES.

We have seen that in order to constitute a *promissory* note it must be for the payment of *money* only; if then a note be payable otherwise than in money, it is called a *chattel* note. Chattel notes are not negotiable, and cannot be sued except in the name of the payee. No days of grace are allowed upon them.

It is the duty of the maker of a chattel note payable in specific articles, at a place mentioned in the note, to *tender* the articles at that place, and at the time the note becomes due. If the maker neglect to make such tender, he will be liable to the payee to pay him the amount

PROMISSORY NOTE.

$95.^{68}/_{100}$

Ninety days after date, for value received, I promise to pay Benjamin Franklin, or bearer, Ninety-five Dollars and Sixty-eight Cents, with Interest.

Lyons, June 18th, 1848.

Jonathan Neverpay.

$157.00

Received, Lyons, February 10th, 1848, of Edmund Hamilton, One Hundred and Fifty-seven Dollars, in full of all demands.

Levi S. Fulton.

of the note in money. But if, on the other hand, the maker tender the articles mentioned in the note, at the proper time and place, according to the contract, and the creditor neglects or refuses to receive them, the debt is thereby discharged; but the right of property in the articles tendered passes to the creditor. The debtor may abandon the goods tendered; but if he elects to retain possession of them, he will be considered as bailee of the creditor at his (the creditor's) risk and expense. The relation of debtor and creditor would in such case be changed to that of bailor and bailee.

There is a difference as to tender between *portable* and *cumbrous* articles. With respect to the former, a tender as above must be made; as to the latter, it will be sufficient if the debtor offer to deliver as the creditor shall direct.

FORMS OF CHATTEL NOTES.

Three months after date, I promise to pay to C. D., or order, one hundred bushels of good merchantable wheat, to be delivered at the residence of said C. D.

A. B.

Rochester, Aug. 1, 1848.

$75.

Four months from date, I promise to pay to C. D., or bearer, at my place of residence in this city, seventy-five dollars' worth of sound and merchantable winter apples.

A. B.

Rochester, August 1, 1848.

CHECKS ON BANKS AND BANKERS.

A Check is a written order addressed to a bank, or to persons carrying on the business of bankers, by a person having money in their hands, requesting them to pay to another person, or to his order, a certain sum of money mentioned in the check.

Checks differ from Bills of Exchange in the following respects:

1st. They are always drawn on a bank, or on bankers, and are payable immediately on presentment, without any days of grace.

2d. They require no acceptance as distinct from payment.

3d. They are always supposed to be drawn upon a previous deposit of funds.

In order to make the drawer liable, in case the check is dishonored, the holder must present it for payment within a reasonable time, and if dishonored, must give the drawer notice thereof within a reasonable time also.

CHECK.

August 1, 1848.

Cashier Rochester City Bank, pay H. M. Richardson, or bearer, two thousand five hundred dollars.

R. L. Brayton.

$2,500.

RECEIPTS.

A receipt in full, though strong evidence, is not conclusive; and a party signing such receipt will be permitted to show a mistake or error therein, if any exist.

Receipts for the payment of money are open to examination, and may be varied, explained, or contradicted, by parol testimony.

GENERAL FORM OF A RECEIPT ON ACCOUNT.

$50.

Rochester, August 1, 1848.

Received of C. D. fifty dollars, to apply on his account.

A. B.

RECEIPT IN FULL.

$110.10.

Rochester, August 1, 1848.

Received of C. D., one hundred ten dollars and ten cents, in full of all demands against him.

A. B.

RECEIPT FOR MONEY PAID BY THIRD PERSONS.

$100.

Rochester, August 1, 1848.

Received of C. D., by the hand of E. F., one hundred dollars, to apply on account of said C. D.

A. B.

RECEIPT FOR MONEY ON BOND.

$200.

ROCHESTER, August 1, 1848.

Received of C. D. two hundred dollars, to apply on his bond, dated the —— day of ———, 18—, being the same sum this day endorsed on said bond.

A. B.

RECEIPT FOR INTEREST MONEY.

$140.

ROCHESTER, August 1, 1848.

Received of C. D. one hundred and forty dollars, being the annual interest due on his bond, dated the —— day of ———, 18—, given to me (or to E. F.), and conditioned for the payment of the sum of ——— dollars in —— years from date, with annual interest.

A. B.

RECEIPT TO BE ENDORSED ON BOND.

$140.

ROCHESTER, August 1, 1848.

Received of C. D. one hundred and forty dollars, being the annual interest due on the within bond, and the same sum this day receipted by me to the said C. D.

A. B.

RECEIPT FOR A NOTE OF THIRD PERSON.

ROCHESTER, August 1, 1848.

Received of C. D. a promissory note against E. F. (dated April 4th, 1847, and on which there is due one hundred dollars), which, when paid, shall be in full of all demands against the said C. D.

A. B

BONDS.

A bond is an acknowledgment, under seal, of a debt, duty, or obligation; and it is immaterial what mode of expression is used, provided the language be sufficient to establish an acknowledgment of a debt.

Every bond, in itself, imports a consideration; and a failure of the consideration is not a good defence to an action brought on the bond. Fraud, however, or an illegal consideration, will invalidate a bond.

Wax, or some other tenacious substance, is necessary in order to make a legal seal, except it be the seal of a court or public officer.

COMMON FORM OF A BOND.

Know all men by these presents, that I, A. B., of the town of ——, in the county of ——, and State of New York, am held and firmly bound unto C. D., of, &c., in the sum of one thousand dollars, lawful money of the United States of America, to be paid to the said C. D., his executors, administrators or assigns; for which payment, well and truly to be made, I bind myself, my heirs, executors and administrators firmly by these presents.

Sealed with my seal. Dated this —— day of ——, one thousand eight hundred and ——.

The condition of the above obligation is such, that if the above bounden, A. B., his heirs, executors or administrators, shall well and truly pay, or cause to be paid unto the above-named C. D., his executors, administrators or assigns, the just and full sum of five hundred dollars, in five equal annual payments from the date hereof, with annual interest, then the above obligation to be void; otherwise to remain in full force and virtue.

Sealed and delivered in the presence of G. H. } A. B. [L. S.]

CHATTEL MORTGAGES.

Every mortgage, or conveyance intended to operate as a mortgage, of goods and chattels, which shall not be accompanied by an immediate delivery and continued change of possession of the things mortgaged, is *absolutely void*, as against the creditors of the mortgagor, subsequent purchasers, and mortgagees in good faith, unless the mortgage, or a true copy thereof, be filed in the office of the clerk of the town where the mortgagor resides at the time of the execution thereof.

Within thirty days next preceding the expiration of a year from the filing a chattel mortgage as aforesaid, a true copy of such mortgage, with a statement exhibiting the interest of the mortgagee in the property mortgaged, should again be filed with such clerk.

After default in the payment of a chattel mortgage, the mortgagee's title to the property mortgaged becomes absolute at law, and he is entitled to the immediate possession thereof.

CHATTEL MORTGAGE.

This indenture, made the —— day of ———, between A. B., of ———, of the first part, and C. D., of ———, of the second part, witnesseth: That the said party of the first part, in consideration of the sum of ——— dollars, to him duly paid, hath sold, and by these presents doth grant and convey to the said party of the second part, the following described goods, chattels, and property (*describe them particularly, or refer to them in the schedule*), now in my possession, at the ——— of ——— aforesaid; together with the appurtenances, and all the estate, title, and interest of the said party of the first part therein.

This grant is intended as a security for the payment of one hundred and ten dollars, with interest, on or before the expiration of one year from the date hereof; and the additional sum of one hundred and forty dollars, with interest, on the —— day of ———, 18—; which payments, if duly made, will render this conveyance void.

In witness whereof the said party of the first part hath hereunto set his hand and seal, the day and year first above written.

Sealed, signed, and delivered in presence of G. H. — A. B. [L. S.]

BILL OF SALE.

A Bill of Sale is a written contract, or agreement, transferring and assigning the ownership of personal property, or any interest in the same. If fraudulent, as against third persons, it is void.

COMMON BILL OF SALE.

Know all men by these presents, that I, A. B., of the town of ———, in the county of ———, and State of New York, of the first part, for and in consideration of the sum of ——— dollars, lawful money of the United States, to me in hand paid, at or before the ensealing and delivery of these presents, by C D., of &c., of the second part, the receipt whereof is hereby acknowledged, have bargained and sold, and by these presents do grant and convey, unto the said party of the second part, his executors, administrators, and assigns (*here state the property sold*), to have and to hold the same unto the said party of the second part, his executors, administrators, and assigns forever. And I do, for myself, my heirs, executors, and administrators, covenant and agree, to and with the said party of the second part, his executors, administrators, and assigns, to warrant and defend the sale of the said property, goods, and chattels, hereby made unto the said party of the second part, against all and every person and persons whomsoever.

In witness whereof I have hereunto set my hand and seal, this —— day of ——, one thousand eight hundred and ——.

Signed, sealed, and delivered in presence of G. H. — A. B. [L. S.]

POWER OF ATTORNEY.

A Letter or Power of Attorney, is a written delegation of authority by which one person enables another to do an act for him.

When a power is special, and the authority limited, the attorney cannot bind his principal by any act in which he exceeds that authority; but the authority of the attorney will be so construed as to include all necessary means of executing it with effect.

When the power is in writing, and subject to the inspection of the party, no good reason exists for binding the principal beyond the scope of it; though in general he who employs an agent or attorney shall lose by his fraudulent or illegal acts, in preference to an innocent third person.

GENERAL FORM OF POWER OF ATTORNEY.

Know all men by these presents, that I, A. B., of ——, in the county of ——, and State of New York, have made, constituted, and appointed, and by these presents do make, constitute, and appoint C. D., of &c., my true and lawful attorney, for me, and in my name, place, and stead, to (*set forth the subject matter of the power;*) giving and granting unto my said attorney, full power and authority to do and perform all and every act and thing whatsoever requisite and necessary to be done in and about the premises, as fully, to all intents and purposes, as I might or could do if personally present, with full power of substitution and revocation, hereby ratifying and confirming all that my said attorney or his substitute shall lawfully do or cause to be done by virtue thereof.

In witness whereof I have hereunto set my hand and seal, this ——— day of ———, in the year one thousand eight hundred and ——.

Sealed and delivered in the presence of G. H. } A. B. [L. S.]

REVOCATION OF A POWER OF ATTORNEY.

Know all men by these presents, that whereas I, A. B., of &c., in and by my letter of attorney bearing date the —— day of ———, in the year one thousand eight hundred and ———, did make, constitute, and appoint C. D., of &c., my true and lawful attorney, for me and in my name, to &c. (*here copy the language of the Letter of Attorney*), as by the said letter will more fully appear: now know ye that I, the said A. B., have revoked, countermanded, annulled, and made void, and by these presents do revoke, countermand, annul, and make void, the said letter of attorney, and all power and authority thereby given, or intended to be given, to the said C. D.

In witness &c. (as in Letter of Attorney).

DEEDS.

All instruments under seal are deeds; but the term "deed" is generally understood as applying to conveyances of land.

The consideration of a deed may either be *good* or *valuable*. A *good* consideration is founded upon natural love and affection between near relations by blood; a *valuable* consideration is founded on something deemed valuable, as money, goods, service, or marriage.

Every deed or contract is void when made for any fraudulent purpose, or in violation of law.

A SIMPLE DEED.

This indenture, made the —— day of ———, in the year of our Lord one thousand eight hundred and ———, between A. B., of &c., of the first part, and C. D., of &c., of the second part, witnesseth: That the said party of the first part, for and in consideration of the sum of ——— dollars, to him in hand paid by the said party of the second part, the receipt whereof is hereby acknowledged, hath bargained and sold, and by these presents doth bargain and sell, unto the said party of the second part, and to his heirs and assigns forever, all (*here describe the premises;*) together with all and singular the hereditaments and appurtenances thereunto belonging, or in anywise appertaining; and the reversion and reversions, remainder and remainders, rents, issues, and profits thereof; and also all the estate, right, title, interest, claim, or demand whatsoever, of him, the said party of the first part, either in law or equity, of, in, and to the above bargained premises, and to every part and parcel thereof: to have and to hold to the said party of the second part, his heirs and assigns, to the sole and only proper use, benefit, and behoof of the said party of the second part, his heirs and assigns forever.

In witness whereof the said party of the first part has hereunto set his hand and seal, the day and year first above written.

Sealed and delivered in presence of G. H. — A. B. [L. S.]

QUIT-CLAIM DEED.

Know all men by these presents, that we, A. B., of, &c., and E., the wife of the said A. B., in consideration of the sum of ———, to us in hand paid by C. D., of, &c., the receipt whereof we do hereby acknowledge, have bargained, sold, and quit-claimed, and by these presents do bargain, sell, and quit-claim unto the said C. D., and to his heirs and assigns forever, all our, and each of our right, title, interest, estate, claim, and demand, both at law and in equity, and as well in possession as in expectancy, of, in, and to all that certain piece or parcel of land situate (*here give description*), with all and singular the hereditaments and appurtenances thereunto belonging.

In witness whereof we have hereunto set our hands and seals, the day and year first above written.

Sealed and delivered in presence of G. H. — A. B. [L. S.]
E. B. [L. S.]

WARRANTY DEED.

To all people to whom these presents shall come, greeting: Know ye that I, A. B., of &c., for the consideration of ——— dollars, received to my full satisfaction of C. D., of &c., do grant, bargain, sell, and confirm unto the said C. D., his heirs and assigns, all (*here give description;*) to have and to hold the above granted and bargained premises, with the appurtenances thereof, unto the said C. D., his heirs and assigns, to his and their own proper use and behoof forever. And I do for myself, and my heirs, executors, and administrators, covenant with the said C. D., his heirs and assigns, that at and until the ensealing of these presents, I am well seized of these premises, as a good and indefeasible estate in fee simple, and have good right to bargain and sell the same, in manner and form aforesaid; and that the same is free from all encumbrance whatsoever.

And further, I do by these presents bind myself, and my heirs, to warrant and forever defend the above granted and bargained premises, unto the said C. D., his heirs and assigns, against all claims and demands whatsoever.

In witness whereof I have hereunto set my hand and seal, the —— day of ———, in the year one thousand eight hundred and———.

Sealed and delivered in presence of G. H.

A. B. [L. S.]

MORTGAGE.

This Indenture, made the —— day of ———, in the year of our Lord one thousand eight hundred and ———, between A. B., of &c., of the first part, and C. D. of ———, of the second part, witnesseth: That the said party of the first part, for and in consideration of the sum of ——— dollars, doth grant, bargain, sell, and confirm unto the said party of the second part, and to his heirs and assigns, all (*description;*) together with all and singular the hereditaments and appurtenances thereunto belonging, or in anywise appertaining. This conveyance is intended as a mortgage, to secure the payment of the sum of ——— dollars in ——— years from the date of these presents, with annual interest, according to the conditions of a certain bond, dated this day, executed by the said A. B. to the said party of the second part; and these presents shall be void if such payment be made. But in case default shall be made in the payment of the principal, or interest, as above provided, then the party of the second part, his executors, administrators, and assigns, are hereby empowered to sell the premises above described, with all and every of the appurtenances, or any part thereof, in the manner prescribed by law; and out of the money arising from such sale, to retain the said principal and interest, together with the costs and charges.

9 781425 524692

www.ingramcontent.com/pod-product-compliance
Lightning Source LLC
LaVergne TN
LVHW011201110826
845150LV00006B/1286

* 9 7 8 1 4 2 5 5 1 0 3 0 5 *